THE FUTURE OF TRANSATLANTIC SECURITY RELATIONS

COLLOQUIUM REPORT

Edited by
Richard A. Chilcoat
Joseph R. Cerami
Patrick B. Baetjer

Sponsored by
U.S. Army's Dwight D. Eisenhower National Security Series
U.S. Army War College, Strategic Studies Institute
The European Union Center for Excellence at Texas A&M
University
The George Bush Presidential Library Foundation
The George Bush School of Government and Public Service

September 2006

*****

The views expressed in this report are those of the editors and do not necessarily reflect the official policy or position of the Department of the Army, the Department of Defense, or the U.S. Government. This report is cleared for public release; distribution is unlimited.

*****

This publication is a work of the U.S. Government as defined in Title 17, United States Code, section 101. As such, it is in the public domain, and under the provisions of Title 17, United States Code, Section 105, it may not be copyrighted.

*****

Comments pertaining to this report are invited and should be forwarded to: Director, Strategic Studies Institute, U.S. Army War College, 122 Forbes Ave, Carlisle, PA 17013-5244.

*****

All Strategic Studies Institute (SSI) monographs are available on the SSI home-page for electronic dissemination. Hard copies of this report also may be ordered from our homepage. SSI's homepage address is: *www.StrategicStudiesInstitute.army.mil*.

*****

The Strategic Studies Institute publishes a monthly e-mail newsletter to up-date the national security community on the research of our analysts, recent and forthcoming publications, and upcoming conferences sponsored by the Institute. Each newsletter also provides a strategic commentary by one of our research analysts. If you are interested in receiving this newsletter, please subscribe on our homepage at *www.StrategicStudiesInstitute.army.mil/newsletter/*.

ISBN 1-58487-258-6

CONTENTS

FOREWORD

The George Bush School of Government and Public Service, the European Center of Excellence at Texas A&M University, the George Bush Presidential Library Foundation, the Department of the Army's Eisenhower National Security Series, and the U.S. Army War College's Strategic Studies Institute were proud to sponsor the Future of Transatlantic Security Relations Conference held at the Bush Presidential Conference Center in College Station, Texas, on March 8, 2006. A number of scholars from all over the United States and Europe came great distances to participate in the discussions and seminars. We appreciated their efforts, and I believe we have captured their remarks and ideas faithfully within this conference report.

The Transatlantic Security Relationship has been an anchor of European and U.S. foreign policy since the closing days of World War II. As the conflict drew to a close, a new one rose from its ashes. The Cold War and its many harrowing moments reinforced, time and again, the importance of maintaining close ties and mutual understanding across the ocean—a distance that has grown ever smaller in this age of globalization.

The purpose of the conference was to examine the future of this storied alliance. There were three key objectives. First, we aimed to raise the national security community's awareness and understanding of U.S. and European security relations. Our second goal was education—our efforts sought to contribute to the knowledge of U.S.-European security affairs for faculty and university students from across the Southwestern United States. The last goal was to contribute to current research and publications on U.S.-European affairs by drawing attention to the security challenges the United States currently faces and will face in the near-term future. Our panel discussions, debates, and keynote speeches strove to clarify key conceptual questions, examined current areas of cooperation and conflict, and reviewed defense, foreign, and homeland security policy and strategy, as well as military force transformation issues.

While the multitude of challenges that confront the United States and Europe cannot be solved in one day, our efforts, we believe, contributed substantively to the ongoing discussion about the future of the transatlantic relationship in academia and the policy community. We thank all of our guests, our national security experts, our Bush School and A&M faculty and students, and the distinguished members of the A&M community who joined with us on March 8. Their efforts to address these critical national and international security issues were Herculean, and this conference report strives to encapsulate their many concerns, thoughts, and remarks.

Richard A. Chilcoat
Dean

LETTER FROM PRESIDENT GEORGE H. W. BUSH

Dear Friends,

I am proud that we hosted "The Future of Transatlantic Security Relations Conference" at Texas A&M University, and I am confident that you will find this conference report quite valuable. A number of important viewpoints and ideas were exchanged throughout the day at the Annenberg Conference Center.

More than 10 years ago, Lieutenant General Brent Scowcroft and I recorded the ideas, insights, and events that informed the foreign policy decisions made during my Presidency. We bore witness to truly incredible events, events that inspired the title of our book, *A World Transformed*. Indeed, we wrote, "In a sense, these years concluded nearly three-quarters of a century of upheaval, the tides of totalitarianism, world wars, and nuclear standoff. . . . Paralyzing suspicion had given way to growing trust; confrontation to collaboration." In many ways, no relationship during my Presidency proved more important than the cooperative efforts between the United States, Europe, and Russia during and after the fall of the Berlin Wall.

Fortunately, despite our differences, I believe that we have resisted those who would cast aside the years of cooperation to embark along solitary paths. Fifteen years after we all witnessed truly historic events, this conference afforded us the opportunity to assess the past, present, and future of U.S.-European relations.

I greatly appreciated the efforts of our conference planning team, including Texas A&M University's European Union Center of Excellence, the Bush Presidential Library Foundation, and the Bush School of Government and Public Service. Let me also thank the U.S. Army's Dwight D. Eisenhower National Security Series and the U.S. Army War College's Strategic Studies Institute for their generous sponsorship for this event.

Sincerely,
George H. W. Bush

INTRODUCTION

As former President George H. W. Bush pointed out in the preceding letter,

> In many ways, no relationship during my Presidency proved more important than the cooperative efforts between the United States, Europe, and Russia during and after the fall of the Berlin Wall. Fortunately, I believe that despite our differences, we have resisted those who would cast aside the years of cooperation to embark along solitary paths. Fifteen years after we all witnessed truly historic events, this conference afforded us the opportunity to assess the past, present, and future of U.S.-European relations.

The conference participants' presentations focused on four main questions regarding the future of transatlantic relations: What is the current status of the Atlantic Alliance, and how will long-standing relationships among the United States, Europe, and Russia change in the near term? How will relations between Turkey, the European Union (EU), the United States, and the North Atlantic Treaty Organization (NATO) evolve? Why has NATO and the transatlantic partnership endured and will it continue to do so? and What are NATO's future roles and missions?

Short answers to these complex questions include the following observations that are addressed in more detail in this conference report. First, relations with Russia will depend largely on whether Russia views the enlargement of the EU and NATO as a threat. Second, while the status of its application is still pending, U.S. and European relations with Turkey will, of course, depend heavily on whether it is admitted to the EU in full member status. Third, NATO has endured largely because, as an international institution, it has deep and enduring value as illustrated in the concept of "stickiness," which is addressed in this report's concluding section. Finally, NATO will play a variety of new roles and missions, but it will never again resemble its original design as a Cold War conventional warfighting organization.

PANEL 1: FORCE STRUCTURE AND POWER PROJECTION FOR THE REGION AND BEYOND

Defense Transformation: Impact on Transatlantic Relations

Repositioning U.S. Forces: Strategic and Operational Dimensions

European Views: The Impact of Transformation and Repositioning on Europe, NATO, and Regional Security.

Chair: Dr. Jeffrey Engel, Bush School of Government and Public Service, Texas A&M University

Members:
   Colonel William J. Gallagher, Commanding General's Initiative Group, U.S. Army, Europe and 7th Army
   Dr. Alan P. Dobson, Director, Institute for Transatlantic European and American Studies, The University of Dundee, Scotland
   Dr. Jay Lockenour, Department of History, Temple University

Summary of Colonel Gallagher's main points. To begin, Colonel Gallagher referred to the remarks made by U.S. Secretary of Defense Donald Rumsfeld at the 42nd Conference on Security Policy in Munich on February 3-5, 2006. He stressed that the goal of many Islamic terrorists is the establishment of a caliphate that would stretch across many borders. This transnational threat, therefore, requires a collective transnational response, which is why the United States relies heavily on the North Atlantic Treaty Organization (NATO) in the Global War on Terror (GWOT).

Beyond terrorism, Colonel Gallagher pointed to several security issues where cooperation between the United States and Europe is vital. Overall, he stated that the Balkans was a NATO success story, and that the alliance may grow, with Croatia and Macedonia now eligible for membership. In Eurasia, he pointed to the Ukraine as an important regional ally and stressed the importance of continued European Union (EU)-U.S. support for the country. In the South

Caucuses, Georgia is emerging as a significant ally, even sending troops to support the coalition in Iraq. With regard to Russia, Colonel Gallagher suggested that military-to-military relations were quite good, with the U.S. and Russian militaries having recently completed 14 cooperative exercises, with an additional 13 being planned.

In Africa, however, there are a number of problems that require greater EU-U.S. cooperation. The continent is subject to extreme poverty, harsh climates, extremism, and ethnic conflict. Colonel Gallagher saw one of the most important goals in West Africa as being the professionalization of those countries' militaries, making them subordinate to civilian leadership and not partisan, ethnicity-driven forces. In central Africa, there remains much work to be done. He pointed to Operation ENDURING FREEDOM TRANS-SAHARA as an ongoing effort to eliminate the ungoverned areas where criminal and terrorist elements might try to take root.

Colonel Gallagher's focus then shifted to the transformation of the U.S. military in Europe. He explained that transformation refers to the efforts to make the U.S. military more modular, flexible, and lethal for use in both humanitarian operations and conventional war. Some asked why the U.S. military even is needed in Europe. He asserted that there are operational and strategic reasons. Operationally, Europe has good infrastructure and is geographically closer to many of the regions that the U.S. military operates in. Therefore, Europe remains an important power projection platform for U.S. forces. Second, and more important, coalitions are the best way to combat today's conventional and terror threats. The interaction of the U.S. and European militaries on the continent plants the seeds for future coalitions. They have established means of interaction. Gallagher did mention, however, that the United States would like to increase the interoperability between its forces and Europe's.

Colonel Gallagher pointed out that Secretary Rumsfeld's program to achieve this defense transformation has included sending U.S. heavy equipment home and shrinking the U.S. footprint in Germany, while seeking basing rights south of the Alps and in the Black Sea region. The idea is to have a less heavy permanent force structure, with only a modularized airborne unit in Italy and a Stryker-equipped maneuver brigade in Germany. As currently planned, units will rotate every 6 months out of the United States and into the Black Sea region for training purposes. The impact on European regional security is significant; the unit rotational approach reduces the capability gap between allies, allows NATO more command and control over NATO forces, and makes available more U.S. units for redeployment or rotation missions.

In closing, Colonel Gallagher mentioned the importance of the training that the United States provides to the Eastern European officer corps. He stated that the young U.S. noncommissioned officers are vital to the effectiveness of the U.S. military. Furthermore, he commented on the improving relationship between the United States and Germany. The reason is three-fold: a shared threat in Iran; the change in political leadership with the election of Angela Merkel; and the U.S. commitment to reduce its footprint in Germany.

Summary of comments by Dr. Dobson. Dr. Dobson began by reiterating his belief that a special relationship exists between the United States and Great Britain. He then suggested that there is a sense of some sort of challenge to this relationship. Simply stated, the question is: With the end of the Cold War, what is the purpose or the *raison d'etre* of the relationship? Dr. Dobson suggested that perhaps the alliance had always been more than a simple, realist arrangement with overlapping values. He then discounted the notion that the relationship consisted merely of geopolitical concerns blended with overlapping values, pointing to disparities between the United States and the UK. The gap in gross domestic product (GDP) between the two continues to grow, there is a massive difference in the military capabilities of each, and U.S. Secretary of Defense Rumsfeld had slighted the British by suggesting that their troops were not needed in Iraq.

So what underpins the U.S.-UK relationship? Dr. Dobson pointed out that such questions are not new. Realist concerns and overlapping values are not the answer. The strains on the relationship brought on by the Suez Crisis and the Cuban Missile Crisis did reveal, however, that narrower national interests can trump the alliance. In addition, Dr. Dobson suggested that values can change dramatically, but are impotent if the political will to act on them does not exist. In short, the relationship between the United States and the UK has been close since the 1930s. Dr. Dobson asserted that British foreign policy has stressed the twin goals both of being able to act on its own and being interoperable with U.S. forces. Intelligence has been one area of ongoing cooperation; for example, an American representative sits on the British Joint Intelligence Committee. This arrangement would be difficult to disentangle even if both sides wanted to.

Dr. Dobson then highlighted a number of other areas of cooperation. In 2004, the United States agreed to allow the UK to purchase newer nuclear delivery systems. The UK gets early warning of a nuclear strike via radar and signals intelligence-gathering facilities that are shared readily with the United States. The Royal Air Force and the U.S. Air Force train together regularly on an informal basis. Dr. Dobson cautioned, however, that the current relationship cannot be maintained in its present form over time if the British continue to be portrayed as a "poodle" to the United States. He acknowledged that the Bermuda Mutual Airspace Agreement was an unfettered victory for British interests, but that there has to be more equitable compromises between the two nations if the special relationship is to continue to mean anything. His view is that France has proven to be a big threat to British/EU collaboration with the United States, in that the French would like to establish an independent European security force capable of acting without assistance from the United States.

Dr. Dobson then focused on NATO. The United States and the UK seem to want NATO to be the dominant European security force with an out-of-area capability. Europeans are shouldering more of the NATO burden as evidenced by the commitments in Afghanistan, but the United States would like to exercise more influence at the EU table. The administration of George W. Bush, Dr. Dobson asserts, has made wielding such influence more difficult by declaring its right to act unilaterally, promulgating a doctrine of preventative war, and declaring the existence of universal values. British Prime Minister Tony Blair is being pressured heavily to keep NATO at the forefront of European security force discussions, although, Dr. Dobson pointed out, Blair launched the Common Foreign and Defense Policy (CFDP) in 1998 with French Prime Minister Chirac and appeared to have a very different view at that time. Since 2002, the United States has supported a NATO rapid-reaction force in an attempt to undermine calls for an independent European reaction force. Dr. Dobson acknowledged that out-of-area NATO operations are increasing, and suggested that the United States values NATO for helping to combat terrorism and protect strategic regions.

Dr. Dobson stated that the tensions in the U.S./UK/European relationship are not new, and that the underlying interests are themselves not new. There has been some progress with the firm anchoring of many of the former Soviet satellites into the EU and/or NATO and the fact that NATO invoked NATO's Article 5 for the first time following the attacks of September 11, 2001 (9/11). Overall, cooperation between the British and the United States is vital in order to moderate France's vision of the CFDP. Realism and neoliberalism provide little illumination for a path forward. A pragmatic, ad hoc approach between the United States, UK, and Europe is necessary.

Summary of Dr. Lockenour's main points. Dr. Lockenour reflected that there has been an overwhelming number of people who have thought about the future, come to conclusions, and been completely wrong. History, he maintained, is not a predictive discipline. Each generation has thought that it lived in a particularly challenging time or unique time. Given the tendency to see current events as uniquely difficult, predicting the future thus becomes more dangerous or uncertain.

Dr. Lockenour stated that though history is not predictive, there are a number of continuities that can be traced from the past to today. For instance, politics is still a vital component of the transatlantic relationship, although politics can change dramatically. In Germany, the Christian Democrats historically have been comfortable with a close relationship with the United States. The election of Christian Democrat leader, Angela Merkel, and her subsequent comments, suggest that Germany will seek a more amicable relationship with the United States than was pursued by Gerhard Schröder.

With regard to force transformation, Germans have seen this taking place since 1990 with the gradual integration of the East and West German militaries. Germans remain concerned that the army could one day be a threat to democracy, a deep psychological hangover from World Wars I and II, and thus have preferred a form of democratic leadership within the military. Universal military service is seen as an additional measure that restrains the military.

Having cautioned the audience on the utility and effectiveness of making predictions, Dr. Lockenour outlined the broad themes that he believed would define the transatlantic relationship in the future. First, NATO has been and will continue searching for a role in the post-Cold War world. Second, the stationing of thousands of U.S. troops in Europe and Germany produced a special relationship, a bond that will continue into the future.

Questions.

Question: Unknown speaker asked Colonel Gallagher to describe in greater detail the U.S. plans for the Black Sea Region.

Answer: Colonel Gallagher responded that the troops deployed in the Black Sea region could be either active or reserve troops, and that Romania and Bulgaria were likely candidates for hosting the troops. The deployed force will be a brigade in size, meaning that the U.S. European Command will have three brigades, or 25,000 troops, at any given time. The United States will be moving away from regionally based forces, and move to expeditionary forces modeled on the 82nd Airborne support of the U.S. Central Command (CENTCOM).

Comment: Mr. Klaus-Peter Gottwald, the Deputy Chief of Mission for the German Embassy in Washington, DC, stated that there has been conflict within Germany over what area will be chosen to station the Strykers and which area will see a decline in the presence of U.S. troops. He pointed out that, while Germany opposed the invasion of Iraq, it allowed the United States to utilize the bases in Germany to support its operations. Mr. Gottwald disagreed with Dr. Lockenour's suggestion that the Social Democrats were less welcoming to the United States than the Christian Democrats.

Question: Ms. Oya Dursun, Ph.D. candidate from Texas University: Could the panel address the political implications of redeployment of U.S. forces?

Answer: Dr. Alan Dobson replied that at the heart of the issue is the concern that European and U.S. security issues are not the same. The second problem is that the European militaries cannot keep pace with the technological advancements of the U.S. military and have interoperability issues. European civilians are not willing to make the sacrifices necessary to boost European warmaking capabilities and interoperability. The British have tried to open up the acquisition process in order to drive costs down through competition, but they have been only marginally successful.

Question: Dr. Michael Brenner suggested that the creation of the European Rapid Reaction Force (ERRF) was aimed at giving Europeans greater influence in joint operations.

Answer: Dr. Lockenour acknowledged Dr. Brenner's point, but suggested that the ERRF and the European Security and Defense Policy are flawed fundamentally because the Europeans cannot speak with one voice on issues of defense and security.

Dr. Dobson added that the Bush administration's 2002 *National Security Strategy Statement* declaring the right of the United States to engage in preemptive war deeply worries Europeans.

Colonel Gallagher expressed considerable reservations about the creation of a ERRF. He suggested that the creation of multiple armies for multiple missions would decrease NATO's capabilities.

PANEL 2: OVERVIEW OF TRENDS, THEMES, AND GRAND STRATEGY

Understanding Emerging Trends and Themes in Transatlantic Relations: A U.S. View

Understanding Emerging Trends and Themes in Transatlantic Relations: A European View

Grand Strategies: Converging and Diverging Forces, and the Opportunities for Building Consensus.

Chair: Dr. Michael Desch, The Bush School of Government and Public Service, Texas A&M University.

Members:

- Dean James B. Steinberg, Lyndon B. Johnson School of Public Affairs, The University of Texas at Austin
- Dr. Guillaume Parmentier, French Center on the United States (CFE), Institut Français, Des Relations Internationales (IFRI), France
- Dr. Christopher Layne, The Bush School of Government and Public Service, Texas A&M University

Summary of Dean Steinberg's remarks. Dean Steinberg acknowledged that scholars on the first panel looked at the long history of the transatlantic relationship throughout the Cold War and declared that he would focus primarily on the last 5 1/2 years. He suggested that there are two schools of thought regarding the future of the transatlantic relationship. One sees the various disagreements between Europe and the United States as a passing consequence of the 9/11 terrorist attacks in New York, Pennsylvania, and Washington, DC. The other maintains that a fundamental rift between the United States and Europe opened up, one that would have developed eventually, no matter what.

Dr. Steinberg stated that there appeared to be elements of truth within each, but that the disagreements were fuelled by decisions made and language used by the Bush administration. In recent months, however, the administration has improved in this area. The problem, he maintained, was that Bush campaigned on a traditional foreign policy agenda and emphasized the importance of the traditional U.S. alliances, suggesting that the transatlantic relationship would remain an important alliance. Yet, following the 9/11 attacks, the United States failed to take a global approach and did not reach out for a global consensus, a global strategy, on how to fight terrorism.

In the post-9/11 world, the United States exhibited a different threat perception than its European counterparts and followed different responses as well. Dean Steinberg asserted that the encounter between U.S. Secretary of Defense Donald Rumsfeld and German Foreign Minister Joschka Fischer on February 8, 2003, at the NATO Munich conference, was one of the most troubling moments in the history of the transatlantic relationship. He stated, however, that some rapprochement had occurred, with Rumsfeld giving a relatively conciliatory speech sometime after the incident.

So are we back to the good old days? Dean Steinberg concluded that the Bush administration now sees the value of allies, backing the EU's negotiations with Iran (actually conducted by the so-called EU3 group of Great Britain, Germany, and France), supporting European efforts in Lebanon, Ukraine, and Russia, and backing European measures to combat terrorism.

The difficulty remains that the United States and Europe do not have a sense of a compelling need for cooperation, thus even the smallest differences tend to divide them. For example, when the arms embargo against China was nearly lifted, there was virtually no cooperation between Europe and the United States on how to address the matter. Dean Steinberg acknowledged that Javier Solana, the EU High Representative for the Common Foreign and Security Policy (CFSP), has tried to marry European and American security interests once more.

Summary of Dr. Parmentier's main points. Dr. Parmentier critiqued the current state of the transatlantic relationship. After 2003, he suggested that realism made a comeback. The United States realized that it needed allies in Europe, and Europeans realized that a divided Atlantic made for a divided Europe. Both the United States and Europe recognize the importance of the United Nations (UN), particularly given shared concerns over Iran's nuclear ambitions.

There are, however, deep differences. Europe and the United States see the founding moment of U.S.-European security relations today though entirely different lenses. For Europe, the founding moment was November 11, 1989, when nearly 200 years of European conflict came to an end. No longer was history to be driven by the expansionist goals of whichever European nation was in its ascendancy at the time. Threats were no longer to a nation's territorial integrity; they were much more complicated. But for the United States, the founding moment was September 11, 2001. Dr. Parmentier asserted that the United States saw history as progressing in the wrong direction as it believed it had become less secure.

Furthermore, he suggested that Europeans do not believe in many U.S. justifications for intervention in the Middle East. In sum, Europeans do not believe in a greater Middle East, and though the United States and European views converged on Iran, their diagnoses are much different. To Europe, Iran's nuclear dabbling is a regional problem. To the United States, it is a regime problem, suggesting a whole different set of responses. Dr. Parmentier asserted that Europe sees little use in isolating the Iranian regime, arguing that in Cuba, such isolation just reinforced the regime. Ironically, the rest of the world sees the United States and Europe as one and the same, that is, as countries that try to dictate the behavior of the Third World.

It is imperative, he stated, for the United States and Europe to work together. The United States should "empower" Europe not only because the two entities face the same problems, but because Europe will be involved more deeply in solving the problems. Yet the requisite institutions for such an empowerment are missing. Dr. Parmentier declared that NATO is stuck in the Cold War mentality, and that the political and military sides keep trying to do the other's job. With regard to NATO as a vehicle of empowerment, the United States has been less than enthusiastic, in effect rejecting assistance when Article 5 was invoked for the first time on September 12, 2001. The difficulty is that the United States believes that the mission should define the coalition, whereas Europe prefers permanent alliances. To bridge this gap, he argued, NATO should see its role as a coalition-enabling organization, bringing together the United States and European nations on issues they agree on. NATO should not seek a role that it cannot fill—for instance, Dr. Parmentier is against the use of NATO in Darfur, Sudan. Finally, he argued that a new European-U.S. institution should be created in order to foster cooperation to face today's challenges. This cooperation would be helped, Parmentier asserted, if the leadership void he sees on both sides of the Atlantic were filled.

Summary of Dr. Layne's main points. Dr. Layne resurrected Dean Steinberg's opinion that there are two prevailing views of the transatlantic alliance, one that the United States and Europe have muddled through their differences, and the other that they are drifting apart. He stated that he believed the latter to be the case.

The reason for the U.S.-European divergence, in Dr. Layne's view, is not Iraq or a lack of shared values, but rather that the international system has changed with huge consequences. Fundamentally, he argued, the United States and Europe do not need one another like they once did. There is a far greater incentive for the Europeans to try to counterbalance American hegemony than to remain close allies.

The traditional view is that the United States has been an offshore counterbalance to anyone who sought hegemony over Europe. If that is still the case, then it makes little sense for U.S. troops to remain in Europe. Dr. Layne argued that the Soviet Union was never the driving force behind the U.S. presence in Europe. Rather, the United States wanted to impose its hegemony on the European continent. Former U.S. Secretary of State Dean Acheson made this clear when he explained that the U.S. presence was meant to "keep the United States on top, keep the Germans down, keep the Europeans from killing each other, and to prevent the Europeans from uniting and forming a third way." Acheson also suggested that economic concerns were behind the U.S. footprint as well.

Dr. Layne pointed out that Europe had tried to resist, as seen by Britain's behavior over the last 50 years, as well as France's behavior. French President Charles de Gaulle built a nuclear arsenal despite American opposition and resisted the 1963 Test Ban Treaty.

In the future, Dr. Layne hypothesized, some subset of European countries will build their own military. The discussions about a European Rapid Reaction Force and the Common Security and Defense Policy are a harbinger of future events. The Europeans have not forgotten that they were incapable of dealing with the Kosovo crisis without the U.S. military. In the final analysis, NATO is an instrument of U.S. hegemony. The United States should return to its traditional role as offshore counterbalance to any who would seek to assert hegemony over Europe.

Questions.

Comments: Panelists asked permission from the chair to respond to Dr. Layne.

Dr. Alan Dobson questioned whether the United States is actually a hegemon, as well as Dr. Layne's assertion that the U.S. stationed troops in Europe only to impose its hegemony. Dean Steinberg agreed with Dr. Dobson, suggesting that perhaps a small cadre within the Bush administration was pushing for U.S. hegemony, but that the American public was against it.

Dr. Parmentier dubbed Dr. Layne's views as "Gaullist." He asserted that hegemony requires both the ability and desire to "be on top," and that the United States has shown itself to be the reluctant dominant power. Dr. Parmentier expressed concern that the French left would fashion conspiracy theories out of Dr. Layne's views.

Dr. Layne addressed Dean Steinberg's comments by asserting that there is a huge difference between the U.S. foreign policy elite and public opinion. Furthermore, he was confident that recently declassified documents confirm that the United States made heading off peer competitors a policy during the Cold War.

Question: The panel was asked several questions at once in the interests of time. Colonel Bass asked about Europe's demographic trends, which indicate a rapidly aging population and few young workers to support the social welfare system. Mr. Rad van den Akker, from the Political Affairs and Security Policy Division at NATO headquarters, asked how Europe could integrate Ukraine without angering Russia. Dr. Michael Brenner inquired as to what the practical implications of democracy promotion were for Europe. Mike Abshire suggested that Europe was not monolithic in all of its views, and asked panel members whether or not they believed that Europe's views on Iran were mistaken. Dr. Plamen Pantev, the Director of the Institute for Security and International Studies in Bulgaria, inquired as to how the United States and Europe could overcome their different security outlooks. Mr. Gottwald queried the panel on how the North Atlantic community would deal with the issue of nuclear weapons in the future, suggesting that the global community had moved from nonproliferation to a "nuclear limited license privilege."

Answer: Dean Steinberg replied that with regard to Ukraine, the United States would risk alienating Russia in order to consolidate the gains made in the country. This would be relatively easy for the United States and would come at little cost. The question remains, however, as to how Europe and Russia view the expansion of the EU. It remains unclear how threatened Russia feels by EU expansion, and whether or not there is much enthusiasm for continued EU expansion at the moment. Democratization, he argued, has been met with skepticism in Europe and in the United States. His sense was that both publics were starting to turn against the idea that the spread of democracy should be a U.S. foreign policy objective. Dean Steinberg predicted that the U.S. Congress would seek some sort of third way between strict adherence to nonproliferation as U.S. policy and the nuclear license, as described by Mr. Gottwald. He stressed that it was imperative for there be a strong domestic debate about these issues in the United States.

Answer: Dr. Parmentier acknowledged that Europe's demographics were troubling and that Europe is not monolithic in its views. He returned to his empowerment theme, asserting that the United States must not be or be seen as antagonistic towards European military involvement in joint operations or areas of mutual interest. He suggested that the United States does not like long overseas deployments, and that in future operations the United States would take the lead and then turn it over to Europe, which has demonstrated a greater willingness to wait things out. Vital to such an arrangement, however, is greater planning on the part of the United States. Democracy promotion is problematic. He asked rhetorically what means would be used for such a campaign. Dr. Parmentier asserted that one could either use force, which he indicated was unlikely to be successful, or one could use an information campaign similar to what was used during the Cold War. He declared that such a campaign would be something both the United States and Europe could agree upon. Lastly, he addressed the unspoken question of whether Europe was "breaking apart." In his view, it was not drifting apart but had just pushed too hard, too quickly to integrate such a large number of states. It will take Europe years to be a real actor on the world stage, but consolidation is necessary in order to be a credible partner.

LUNCHEON ADDRESS

Summary.

Major General Robert Ivany (USA-Ret.) shared a personal account of traveling to Hungary in November 1990 to oversee the democratization of the nation's armed forces. The assignment had added significance as the general's parents had fled from Hungary in 1945 to escape the advance of Soviet troops. He pointed out that the Hungarians expressed their desire to turn their military into one that resembled the U.S. military. They had given extensive thought to the philosophical reasons for having an army and had produced a white paper that sought to compare Hungary's situation to that of Switzerland, or NATO countries, in order to gain insight as to the correct path to follow. The Hungarian officers told General Ivany that they wanted to join NATO—a prospect that seemed quite a ways away to him. Yet 4 or 5 years later, Hungary had become a NATO member that contributes substantially today, even assisting the United States as a member of the coalition in Iraq. General Ivany concluded that transformation of society can happen far sooner than expected if the populace embraces it and if the government seizes upon that desire. In the case of Hungary, the Western style of government appealed strongly to its citizens, bringing about monumental change very quickly.

PANEL 3. HOMELAND SECURITY AND TERRORISM

The Atlantic Storm Exercise: Learning Lessons

Homeland Security: U.S. and European Views.

Members:

Dr. David McIntyre, The Bush School of Government and Public Service, TAMU

Colonel Randall J. Larsen, USAF (Retired), Director of the Institute of Homeland Security, Washington, DC.

Mr. Klaus-Peter Gottwald, Deputy Chief of Mission, Embassy of Germany, Washington, DC

Dr. Daniel Hamilton, Center for Transatlantic Relations, the Paul H. Nitze School of Advanced International Studies, Johns Hopkins University

Summary of exchanges between Dr. McIntyre, Colonel Larsen, Mr. Gottwald, and Dr. Hamilton. Colonel Larsen began the third panel by asserting that the outbreak of pandemic flu is more likely in the next 10 years than a biological terrorist attack. He had developed a simulation entitled "Dark Winter" which simulated a smallpox attack on three U.S. cities. Prominent former government officials played leading roles at the relevant agencies. The decisionmakers quickly realized that they did not even know the right questions to ask in such a situation. Larsen declared that the 21st century will be known as the century of biology. Pathogens are not simply local, state, or even national problems—they are indeed global. Countries cannot seal the borders from pathogens. Were pandemic flu to break out, economic activity would virtually cease. The disturbing fact is that a terrorist could purchase the equipment on the Internet needed to manufacture such an organism with as little as $50,000.

Dr. Hamilton explained that they had taken the "Dark Winter" simulation one step further by creating the simulation "Atlantic Storm," which envisioned the pandemic flu crossing the Atlantic to Europe. In this simulation, former officials from the United States and various European countries played the roles of heads of state and heads of relevant organizations. The idea was to expand the strategic challenges so as to embrace the international community. Dr. Hamilton observed that participants were not sure if there had actually been an attack, and they quickly discovered that there were only 700 million doses of the smallpox vaccine. Debates over how to prioritize dosage allocations among countries paralyzed the participants.

Mr. Gottwald, a player in the simulation, remarked that leadership proved vital, and that the problem could not be dealt with simplistically. Dr. Hamilton commented that there was no mechanism for sharing the vaccine, and that the only time Article 5 of the UN Charter had been invoked was after the 9/11 attacks, in response to a security issue within the United States. It was not clear that invoking Article 5 in the simulation would have any meaningful effect. Participants asked whether NATO was the right organization through which to handle the crisis, and disagreements broke out over whether diluting the vaccine to make more doses available was feasible. Dr. Hamilton discussed the advantages and perils of "ring" vaccinations, meaning vaccinating everyone ringing the outbreak site, versus mass vaccination.

The panelists remarked that biodeterrence, the concept that a would-be attacker is limited in what biological agent he can use because he wants to survive the attack, may be in jeopardy, given the willingness of various terror groups to commit suicide. The simulations revealed that one nation's weak points become weak points for its neighbors. Thus questions remain about how a nation can actually "protect" itself from a biological agent. The panel concluded that the United States and Europe needed to reorient themselves to face new threats, and that advanced, integrated planning was desperately needed.

PANEL 4: REALIGNING AMERICAN FORCES IN EUROPE: DEMISE OR REBIRTH OF THE ATLANTIC ALLIANCE?

Comparative Views from the United States and Europe: Opportunities and Obstacles

Is Consensus Possible?

Members:
- Dr. Johan Lembke, Director, EU Center of Excellence and the Bush School of Government and Public Service, TAMU
- Dr. Michael Brenner, Graduate School of Public and International Affairs, University of Pittsburgh
- Dr. Plamen Pantev, Director, Institute for Security and International Studies, Sofia, Bulgaria
- Mr. Rad van den Akker, Political Affairs and Security Policy Division, NATO
- Ms. Oya Dursun, Ph.D. Candidate, Department of Government, the University of Texas at Austin

Summary of Dr. Lembke's Statements. Dr. Lembke framed the discussion by stating that the U.S. realignment with Eastern European countries is advantageous to the United States in that it offers attractive basing closer to areas of operation, it reaffirms the U.S. commitment to its newer allies, and it enables the United States to provide training to the host countries' militaries. It was therefore no surprise that much of the "Coalition of the Willing" was comprised of Eastern European countries where the United States either had a military presence or was seeking one.

Summary of Mr. Akker's main points. Mr. Akker declared that the realignment issue was dead at NATO. The organization saw realignment as a given, logical step that fit well into both the United States and NATO's modernization plans. Furthermore, he acknowledged that commitment to a country was no longer defined by the presence of troops on its soil. The year 2003 was an obvious low point in the alliance with the dispute over the Iraq War, but he

25

believes that NATO has rebounded strongly and that it remains a sound framework for addressing mutual concerns. The rebound was assisted by the fact that President Bush went before the EU and NATO after the Iraq invasion, a sign which was taken as rapprochement in Europe.

Europe and the United States face a number of serious challenges, ranging from terrorism and crime to disease and an aging population. Mr. Akker affirmed that the United States and Europe could not return to their Cold War relationship but needed to engage in a new dialogue. While the EU has a role, NATO should be the key forum for adapting old frameworks. NATO has and will be involved in stabilization missions, but it cannot be just a troop provider, it must be involved on the political side as well. Mr. Akker suggested that NATO would be a good place to hold a dialogue on the problems and future of the Middle East and North Africa (MENA) region.

Mr. Akker pointed out that 19 of 26 NATO countries also are members of the EU. Yet NATO is necessary in order to keep a strategic partnership that eliminates needless competition among European states. This is not to say that the transatlantic dialogue should move solely to the EU. Both the EU and NATO should be utilized. Two important features that set NATO apart from the EU are that it has the capacity to respond militarily to a problem if need be, and that the United States sits at the NATO table as a full member, whereas it certainly does not at the EU. Mr. Akker readily agreed that the dialogue between NATO countries and the United States needs strengthening.

Mr. Akker asserted that NATO's Riga Meeting on April 27-28, 2006, would prove to be an important event. The operations in Kosovo and Afghanistan would be analyzed and reassessed, NATO force transformation would be addressed, to what extent NATO would pursue out-of-area roles would be discussed, and methods for bringing the ANZUS countries and Japan into the alliance would be examined. He stressed that NATO's commitment to both a military and a political platform had to be clearer.

Summary of Dr. Brenner's main points. Dr. Brenner reminded the conference attendees that military alliances historically have endured as long as a threat existed. In the case of the transatlantic alliance, some unraveling surely was expected. And yet the relationship, he declared, had survived in a fairly robust form. Dr. Brenner stated that the United States and Europe are bound together by much more than narrow realist theory interests. The two share values as well as forms of social organization. Despite these shared features, they have not translated to agreement on new missions and security issues. Geography and power projection capabilities led Europe and the United States to come to very different conclusions about threats like terrorism and failed states. The Kosovo mission exhibited unity of consent and mission as a humanitarian intervention, but observers quickly forgot that NATO could not agree that the Balkans were a core mission. The assumption that Kosovo laid the foundations for future operations proved wrong.

Dr. Brenner asserted that the United States and Europe held conflicting views as to the nature of the alliance. It is not, in his view, a conflict over the relative capabilities of Europe as compared to those of the United States. He cited Britain as an example of a European nation with a fairly robust military capability. Instead, it is a crisis of small differences in values and viewpoints. The United States promulgated a preventative war doctrine that Europe is uncomfortable with. The United States has proclaimed that the security of the West is dependent on the global spread of democracy, a belief that is alien to European political elites.

The role of morality in foreign policy is another example of a difference in values. In the United States, morality and a sense of mission are intertwined intimately in foreign policy. The United States views the world as a series of problems to be fixed over time with American ingenuity. Europeans do not see the world in such a manner, and the European sense of identity is not imbued with a sense of mission. They do not believe that the world will eventually emulate the United States. Dr. Brenner declared that Europe is haunted by its history.

Summary of Dr. Pantev's main points. Dr. Pantev viewed the U.S. basing in the Black Sea region as a complement to EU/NATO enlargement and did not see it as a contradiction or an abandonment of the alliance. This was the first time that Bulgaria had the freedom to decide its foreign policy objectives and could think strategically on its own. The bases would allow for greater U.S. involvement in the region.

Exchange. Dr. Brenner argued that the U.S. bases had political meaning and that Europe needed to undergo political and psychological changes in order to develop the will to act. He suggested that European willpower was lacking perhaps because the region had been protected under the American shield for so long. He commented that the ERRF and CSDP were being built employing a "Hindu sense of time."

Dr. Lembke declared that U.S. bases in the Black Sea region would have multiple positive consequences, including stronger trans-atlantic relations, securing European and U.S. energy resources, a counter influence to China and Russia, the strengthening of NATO's southern wing, and a likely increase in foreign direct investment (FDI) in the region.

Dr. Pantev commented that the national perception in Bulgaria is that the country wanted to participate in the war on terror, and that it can provide the United States with geopolitical assistance. Furthermore, Bulgaria has considered the dangers of taking an active role, but it believes it will be a target regardless of whether it acts or not. Bulgaria has the willpower that Western Europe lacks. In terms of security issues, Dr. Pantev explained that Bulgaria is a player for a number of reasons. The western Black Sea coast is becoming increasingly significant, having seen a number of problems including the trafficking of people, drugs, and arms. There is a strong suspicion that terrorists use the region as a transit point or seek to purchase weapons there. With regard to energy security, three major projects traverse Bulgarian territory—the Nabucco, Berganz, and Ambo pipelines.

Summary of Ms. Dursun's main points. Ms. Dursun focused on Turkey's role in NATO and in the EU. Turkey is one of three long-time NATO members that are not in the EU. Ms. Dursun asserted that Turkey is concerned that it will be abandoned by the European Common Security and Defense policy, remarking that admittance to the EU would allay these fears.

The EU would benefit in several ways from admitting Turkey. As a secular state with a Muslim identity, Turkey exerts considerable influence in the Middle East and in the "Stans." It would prove to be a good mediator for European efforts to bring an end to the Israeli/

Palestinian conflict—Turkey wields a great deal of soft power, according to Dursun.

In terms of hard power, Turkey would prove beneficial to the EU should it seek to intervene in an area where there is a substantial Muslim population, because Turks bring a greater awareness of cultural sensitivity as Muslims.

Dursun envisioned Turkey entering the EU as a "privileged partner" but not as a full member. Failure to admit Turkey to the EU in some significant way would prove to be a "deathkiss" for the transatlantic relationship. It also would seem to confirm Samuel Huntington's theory of a clash of civilizations between the West and the Muslim world. She encouraged the United States and Europe to avoid forcing Turkey to choose between the two.

Questions.

Question: What should be done regarding a constitution for the EU?

Answer: Dr. Michael Brenner suggested extracting the best parts of the defunct constitution and consolidating them in a new document.

Question: What are the other panelists' views on Turkey's chances of admittance to the EU, and would a U.S. observer at the EU solve some of the problems mentioned earlier?

Answer: Dr. Plantev feared that the EU might unravel if it got bogged down in exceptional negotiations over Turkey's admittance to the EU. For this reason, he believed that Turkey was unlikely to be offered privileged partner status. In regard to a U.S. observer, Dr. Pantev stated that it would not resolve the differences between the United States and the EU.

KEYNOTE ADDRESS

Text of Dr. Josef Joffe's Remarks, "The Future of Transatlantic Security Relations."

"Whither the Alliance?" This is not a fresh question. Back in the earlier days, it had spawned a major industry on either side of the Atlantic. My generation made quite a nice living with papers and articles whose titles did not begin with the words "Gender, Race, and Class" but rather with "Two Continents Adrift," or with "What Future for NATO?" Trouble was our business, and a thriving one to boot.

Even earlier, in the 1960s when NATO was just a teenager, Henry Kissinger wrote a bestseller called *The Troubled Partnership*. Robert Osgood of the Johns Hopkins School of Advanced International Studies wrote a classic called *Entangling Alliance*. Their epigones went on to write lots of books with "end of the alliance" in their titles, with or without a question mark. All that was decades ago, but, lo and behold, we have gathered here today to address this question once more: Does the Alliance Have a Future?

The message of this excursion into ancient history is the amazing — nay, unbelievable — durability of this longest-lived compact among free nations. Today, the Atlantic Alliance is 57 years old; there has never been anything like it in the history of the nation-state. Not only is this strange animal still around; it keeps expanding. When it was born in 1949, it encompassed ten European and two North American nations. Three years later, Greece and Turkey joined. In 1955, it was West Germany. In 1982, Spain became a member. In 1999, the Czech Republic, Hungary, and Poland — three former enemies — pitched in. Two years ago, the biggest batch of newcomers arrived. These seven countries were Bulgaria, Estonia, Latvia, Lithuania, Romania, Slovakia, and Slovenia. NATO now has 26 members.

Nor is this all. Since the 1990s, the Alliance has acquired a second layer, the Partnership for Peace, which consists of 20 countries ranging from Albania to Uzbekistan. Russia and Ukraine, tied to NATO by special bilateral councils, form the third layer. So NATO now stretches literally around the world: from the East Coast of the United States across the Atlantic, then all the way across Eurasia to the Western Pacific, and thence to San Francisco and Vancouver.

Why do I bore you with these dates and details? To do so is hardly jejune or pedantic. The purpose is to stress the original point, which is not only the longevity but also the vitality of this astounding institution.

Let me make the same point in yet another way. The persistence of NATO can hardly be explained by the absence of crisis; it was never like in the fairy tale where the parties always "lived happily ever after." In fact, NATO is more like a polygamous marriage that persists *in spite of* its myriad crises. At the latest, the Atlantic Alliance should have died a long time ago, sometime after Christmas Day 1991. Why then? Because on that day, the Soviet Union committed suicide by self-dissolution, thus robbing NATO of its reason for being. History and theory tell us that alliances die when they win — when the common foe which gave birth to them and kept them in harness disappears. Yet here we are 15 years later, and NATO is not only around, but bigger than ever.

Let me elaborate. *The most important point is this: The history of the Alliance is the history of its crises.* Start with 1956 when America's oldest allies, Britain and France, invaded Egypt and were forced out and humiliated by the Eisenhower administration. Yet they did not bolt but stayed in. In the same year, the Eisenhower administration proclaimed the "New Look," i.e., a strategy that would substitute tactical nuclear weapons for conventional manpower. This was the "bigger bang for the buck" doctrine, and it turned West Germany, the eastern-most member of NATO, into the foreordained victim of nuclear war; it would be devastated first and foremost. Yet Bonn did not slink off into neutrality.

In the mid-1960s, the Johnson administration scuttled the Multilateral Force (MLF), a fleet of nuclear-armed surface ships, which was to give NATO's non-nuclear members a finger on the trigger. This left a number of European governments, which had gone to bat for the MLF, high and dry, but none of them absconded.

In the late 1970s, the Carter administration pulled a similar stunt. First, it pressed the European allies to accept neutron bombs on their soil. Their governments had to fight a horrifying battle against their anti-nuclear foes, only to wake up one fine day to learn that Jimmy Carter had ditched the deployment. And so it went. In the 1980s, millions of people demonstrated against the deployment of *Pershing II* and cruise missiles, the West German government fell under the assault, and yet the West Europeans did allow those missiles to be deployed on their soil.

Then, again at the latest, NATO should have crumbled during the Second Iraq War of 2003, when only the British truly supported the American war effort, while France and Germany did their worst to torpedo it. But here we are in 2006, and NATO is still around.

The moral of this tale is that there must have been a very powerful glue to keep the alliance together in spite of all these nasty crises. And that glue must have been strong enough to withstand the mightiest alliance killer of them all—victory in war, though it was only a Cold War.

So why didn't the Alliance die its historically foreordained death after the demise of the Soviet Union, whose existence had been NATO's very reason for being? This is such a powerful paradox because an iron law of history tells us that alliances always break up after victory. Here are some examples.

- The all-European alliance that defeated Napoleon at Waterloo in 1815 was dead by 1822, 7 years later, when the Brits went back to their old game of splendid isolation.

- The World War I alliance that vanquished Imperial Germany in 1918 was defunct 1 year later, when the United States absconded.

- By 1922, 4 years after the Great War, the British took a bow, returning to their century-old game of balancing against France, rather than against a resurgent Germany.

- In 1945, the United States and the Union of Soviet Socialist Republics celebrated their common victory over Hitler Germany; 1 year later, the Cold War started, pitting the Western powers against their former Soviet ally.

So alliances do not live very long past victory. Why, then, is NATO still alive? Surely, it should have gone the way of all flesh in 1994 when the last Russian soldier withdrew from Central Europe.

But it did not. In fact, as we have seen, it expanded, which is a true miracle in the history of international politics.

I can think of at least three explanations, which all have a bearing on the future. One is institutions, the second is interests, and the third is innovation.

Institutions.

NATO has always been much more than a traditional alliance that aggregates military strength against a particular enemy. This alliance is so unique because it *denationalized* defense policy. Why do I say this? Remember that NATO is not just a "coalition of the willing," but an *integrated* force with a unified command structure under a single Supreme Commander who is always an American. Integration, for the last 50 years, has shaped habits and above all institutions of cooperation that are absent from a traditional alliance. There are the NATO Council, the Defence Planning Committee, the Nuclear Planning Group, the High Level Group, and so on. Consultation and consensus-building are a permanent way of life in this alliance, and so the institutions of cooperation have become a value in their own right — worth keeping and worth preserving.

In addition, this institution by the name of NATO has been enormously successful in keeping the peace. Peace is good, not only for children and all other living things, but also for alliances because war is a powerful solvent of military coalitions.

In war, when the going gets tough, the not-so-tough go shopping for alternatives. Some opt out because their objectives have been achieved. Others go neutral because they think they will be safer that way, or because it is a lot cheaper to let George do it and carry the brunt of the fighting. You can observe this phenomenon in Iraq right now as one after another nation withdraws from the coalition because permanent victory has proven elusive. But if there is no war, the incentives for bolting do not exist either, and so the status quo endures. Institutions that are not challenged go on forever. The economists have a word for it when they say: "Old taxes are good taxes."

Interests.

What are the interests that provide the glue when the original cement disappears? There are lots of them. One, it is good to have an institution that keeps the United States anchored in Europe because you never know what is lurking down the road—especially to the east where Western Europe is facing a resurgent Russia.

Two, it is good to have the United States in a game where the weaker players do not want to be left alone with the medium-strong like Germany and France. So the United States provides not only a counterweight against a resurgent Russia, but also against these would-be leaders of Europe.

This is why you had that famous split between Old and New Europe during the Iraq war. The farther east you move, the more enthusiastic the newly liberated states of Eastern Europe have been about the United States. It was not in the interest of those closest to Russia to let France and Germany, with Belgium and Luxemburg in tow, to weaken either the United States or the alliance which it leads.

Third, and by no means last, there are no competing security organizations that can carry the burden of leadership and pay the price of security production. The EU has been trying to field a Rapid Reaction Force of 60,000 men for many years now. But the real problem is not manpower; in fact, the EU has more men under arms than the United States.

The real problem is twofold—military and political. With regard to the military dimension, while the EU has the men, it does not have the "money and the ships," as the old 19th-century English ditty had it. When the largest EU member, Germany, spends as much proportionally in GDP terms as Luxemburg, namely 1.5 percent, you know there is a problem of resources. By contrast, the United States spends 4 percent of GDP on its military. As a result, the EU lacks, above all, projection forces: cargo planes, refuelling tankers, troop ships, etc. And so, when individual EU countries intervened in Africa, they had to ask the United States for the logistics.

The EU also lacks the kind of sophisticated weaponry and all the other accoutrements of "network-centric warfare" that allow the United States to fight at a safe stand-off distance. Modern democracies do not like body bags, and so they will go to war only if they can minimize their own casualties. In our days, casualty-avoidance requires lots of stand-off and precision-munitions, which are plentiful only in the American arsenal. Thus European or EU forces have never gone into serious military action without the United States, whether in Bosnia, Kosovo, or Afghanistan. For all its fabulous riches, with an economy the equal of the United States and a population of 450 million, the EU is a piggy-back giant, one that cannot do without the colossus from across the sea. So much for the military side of the ledger.

The second problem is political. Though the EU is way past a common market and by now boasts many features of a federal state, it lacks the coherence and decisiveness to play a role commensurate with its resources. A classic example is the War of the Yugoslav Succession in the 1990s. It unfolded 1 flying-hour from Rome, Munich, and Vienna; it was a series of wars right inside Europe, and yet the EU looked on helplessly as mass mayhem and "ethnic cleansing" took their course. It was only when Clinton's America took the lead — and provided the airpower — that the EU unsheathed its sword against Slobodan Milosevic and Serbia. This is a puzzle with consequences: Why can't Europe even take care of its own back yard? My answer is this: When it comes to the hard issues of security, Europe is still a bunch of separate nation-states rather than a unitary actor, and there is no player in the game strong and legitimate enough to lead the pack.

Sadly, as very recent events showed, the EU cannot even generate the resolve to stand by a member-state under attack — Denmark, which found itself under assault from much of the Islamic world because of some cartoons deemed offensive against the Prophet. Danish embassies were burned, its exports boycotted. Yet there was no united economic and diplomatic response on the part of the others. This little country essentially was left alone.

Europe is big, rich, and populous, but it cannot replace this American-led alliance called NATO. In security affairs, it does not take a "whole village," but a single superpower to make things happen. And so demand for NATO persists, even in the absence of the great foe that once gave rise to it and kept it going.

Innovation.

So far, I have discussed the power of institutions and interests in explaining the longevity of NATO. The third factor is innovation. In the present context, it is better to think of innovation as "supply-side strategy." This is how all institutions, military or business, survive when their original market dwindles. To stress the point again: The moment the last Russian soldier departed from Central Europe, the demand curve for NATO's classical goods shifted rapidly downward. Naturally, companies that lose demand look for new products that can rekindle interest in their wares.

NATO persists in the absence of a powerful foe because it has changed from a single-product business, that is, deterring a Soviet attack, into a multifloor department store.

- On the first floor, there is the traditional stuff: an institution that keeps the habits of cooperation alive and its powder dry against the resurgence of a strategic threat. Call it a kind of *insurance agency* that buys reinsurance from the world's number one underwriter, the United States.

- On the second floor, the Atlantic Alliance offers intervention *capabilities,* where its "unique selling point" (USP), is a multinational force with the kind of firepower, sophistication, and command structures that has no equal in the rest of the world. Certainly, NATO is much better equipped and led than any force the UN has ever been able to field. In the 1990s, NATO applied its military power in two theaters: in Bosnia and in the Kosovo, with successful bombing campaigns against Serbia.

- On the third floor is a kind of *tool shed, where coalitions of the willing are recruited and used.* This is where individual NATO nations, not NATO as such, offer forces either for fighting or for post-combat operations. This is the case, notably, in Afghanistan and the ongoing war in Iraq.

- On the fourth floor are the *stability operations,* designed to keep the peace once the fighting is over. The shelves here are positively brimming with NATO goodies. Several examples will make the point. In 2003, NATO took over the command of ISAF, the Security Assistance Force in Afghanistan. This was the first mission outside Western Europe in history. For 8 years, until 2004, NATO led the International Stabilization Force (SFOR) in Bosnia. NATO still leads KFOR, an international force in charge of maintaining security in the Kosovo. Under Operation ACTIVE ENDEAVOR, NATO has been patrolling the Mediterranean since 9/11 to protect against international terrorism. Finally, NATO is even in Iraq, where it is training Iraqi security forces.

- Let's go to the top floor, my favorite, where NATO offers its most attractive array of wares. Call it *stability export*. Here, the alliance has managed to attract the largest bunch of new customers—all those countries that joined NATO after the collapse of the Soviet Union: Czechia, Hungary, Poland, Bulgaria, Estonia, Latvia, Lithuania, Romania, Slovakia, and Slovenia. All of them have a classic security problem: the nearness of a very large and powerful state with an imperialist history that once owned or dominated them.

But there is more: NATO is the largest and most successful guardian of democracy and stability. Thus, NATO managed to integrate arch-enemies like France and Germany. It managed to do the same to Greece and Turkey. It took in nondemocracies like Portugal and Spain, and provided the kind of haven where authoritarianism eventually lost out to democracy. Today, NATO provides a shelter that stabilizes the young democracies like Bulgaria and Slovakia.

Down the road, I could imagine Bosnia, Serbia, Montenegro, and Albania as members. The Ukraine would join at the drop of a hat. Some visionaries have even broached Israel as a member of the Alliance. In other words, demand for NATO's best product — stability and safety — is strong and soaring. Not bad for a supposed warrior institution that is now in ripe middle age.

Conclusions.

In conclusion, let me return to the original puzzle, which is persistence without a strategic threat. If you look at NATO as a department store or bazaar rather than as a traditional alliance, the puzzle of longevity is not that hard to crack. The three explanations are, as I just elaborated, interests, institutions, and innovation. And that is why this particular alliance cannot be understood in terms of classical alliance theory, whose iron law asserts that alliances lose when they win and die when they prevail.

Let me add, however, that for all its indestructibility in its newly evolved form, the "Classic NATO" — the compact that held the line during the Cold War — is, of course, dead. NATO is no longer the be-all and end-all of Western politics, a role that it played out from 1949 to 1994, the year the last Russian soldiers withdrew from Central Europe. Call it "New NATO," one institution among several who all represent what I would dare call "The Best of the West." Along with the EU, which also is a kind of "empire by invitation," along with the World Trade Organization, the World Bank, the Organization for Economic Cooperation and Development (OECD), the G-8, and a host of subsidiary alliances like the U.S.-Japan Mutual Security Treaty, NATO embodies the postwar liberal and democratic vision that animated U.S. diplomacy during its most creative age. And that's why it stays in business.

It also stays in business because NATO has evolved from a one-trick pony into a multipurpose institution. Its core function, however, remains military security in a world that, alas, has not reached the "End of History." History may be coming to an end only in the sense that great wars between nation-states are becoming rarer. But the frequency of intrastate and nonstate war, i.e., terrorism, is growing by leaps and bounds. After decades of very slow or no nuclear proliferation, nuclear ambitions are soaring. At the same time, the defrocked superpower Russia is back in the global game, followed by new aspirants like China and Iran that used to play second-fiddle in the concert of nations. So it is good to have a tried-and-true security institution like NATO in the game. NATO's enduring attraction is like Mount Everest's: because it is there.

What about the future? Will it always act in common? No. But it can act in ways no other international institution can.

Will it be the world's policeman now that it has globalized its business activities? No, but it is the best multinational police force we have.

Will it continue to expand? Most likely yes.

Will it contract? Most likely no.

Will NATO continue to mute conflicts among its members, as it has done since 1949? I will bet at least even odds that it will.

Will it secure the realm of democracy? For sure.

Would international life be better without it? Definitely not.

Finally, will we meet here again in 5 or 10 years and ask, "Whither the Alliance?" My answer is yes. With all its crises and squabbles, the Alliance reminds me of those two hunters who were flown into Alaska for a week of bear hunting. "Remember," the pilot warns them, "when I am back a week from now to pick you up, only one bear. This plane isn't strong enough to carry two or more." When he returns, there are two dead bears lying on the strip. "Come on," the hunters plead, "we can make it; here is another 300 bucks for your effort." So the plane takes off and crashes 2 minutes later. Both hunters survive. In a daze, one asks the other, "Where are we?" And his buddy replies, "About 100 yards from where we crashed last year."

Of course, they'll come back in following years. Because, like our two hunters, the Alliance won't run out of bears, and it has plenty of planes and ammunition.

CLOSING REMARKS BY DEAN RICHARD A. CHILCOAT

I want to thank all of our participants, but especially our keynote speakers and panel chairs Dr. Jeffrey Engel, Dr. Michael Desch, Dr. Robert Ivany, Dr. David McIntyre, and Dr. Johan Lembke, for helping to frame discussion at the conference.

Thanks to our executive committee and staff, especially Michelle Sullens, Lucero Carranza, Matt Henderson, and Read Deal, who have been involved in this project for over a year.

Thanks again to our sponsors, including the European Center of Excellence at Texas A&M, the George Bush Presidential Library Foundation, the Department of the Army's Eisenhower National Security Series, and the Army War College's Strategic Studies Institute.

The panels covered the realignment of U.S. forces in Europe, homeland security, and terrorism from multiple perspectives, and the trends and themes of U.S. and European grand strategy. While we highlighted numerous challenges and underscored important differences in the European and American perspectives and approaches, I know we took important steps towards fulfilling the goals of this conference in terms of education, research, and outreach for developing a deeper understanding of the transatlantic relationship.

In terms of service and outreach, numerous students and faculty attended the conference panels and keynote speeches. I believe the fruitful discussion so evident in each panel contributed to a deeper understanding by the audience. With regard to research, another conference goal, the panelists were able to share their many years of expertise and research in a collaborative effort to highlight both the conceptual and the technical questions facing the U.S.-European alliance. I am optimistic that the national security community will seriously examine this conference report.

The goal of education, however, will not be filled simply by the publication of this report. It is incumbent upon all of us to take back to our academies and organizations the important lessons and issues brought forward at the conference. In this vein of continuing education, our staff, headed by Professor Joseph Cerami, has made the report available to interested students, faculty, and policymakers around the globe.

As President George H. W. Bush remarked, "The transatlantic relationship has contributed immensely to the prosperity and stability of the entire globe, but we face new challenges every day. We must continue to search for areas of common understanding and cooperative action on both continents."

CONFERENCE PAPERS

Conference participants were given the opportunity to submit a paper or article addressing important issues confronting the transatlantic relationship before and after the conference. Papers include:

Alan P. Dobson, *The Atlantic Alliance and Blair's Pivotal Power: Trying to Make All Things Special;*

Guillaume Parmentier, *How to Avoid a Transatlantic Rift over Iran;*

Randall J. Larsen, *Dark Winter/Atlantic Storm: Key Issues from Two Executive Level Exercises;*

Daniel S. Hamilton and Bradley T. Smith, *Atlantic Storm: Facing the Bioterror Challenge;*

Johan Lembke, *American Realignment in Europe;* and

Patrick B. Baetjer, *Turkey, Russia, and Sticky Institutions: Why the Transatlantic Security Relationship Endures—and Some Thoughts on Future Missions.*

THE ATLANTIC ALLIANCE AND BLAIR'S PIVOTAL POWER: TRYING TO MAKE ALL THINGS SPECIAL

Professor Alan P. Dobson

THE CHALLENGE

Maybe there is a danger of commentators and scholars on both sides of the Atlantic talking the Atlantic Alliance into a more serious situation than it is actually in: a sort of self-fulfilling prophecy brought about by too much concentration on the negative and a lack of more positive and creative imagination.

With the disappearance of Cold War strategic certainties, fractious debates have arisen about the purpose of the Western Alliance, the troubled relationship between the United States and Europe, with Britain often awkwardly placed in between, and particularly NATO and the Common European Security and Defence Policy (CESDP). Back in the early 1990s, within a year of coming into office, President Clinton anticipated some of these problems when he expressed nostalgia for the simple clarities of the Cold War. Its imperatives dictated, among other things, the need for a strong Atlantic alliance, but what was NATO and transatlantic security to be concerned with after the collapse of communism? And what would be the point of the United States allowing the vestiges of some erstwhile special relationship to drag on with Britain? The rationale for a defense alliance appeared to have been removed. Who or what was now likely to challenge either Europe or the United States?

One way of circumventing those questions and of arguing for continuity was to assert that neither NATO nor the Anglo-American special relationship has ever been a realist-driven arrangement exclusively obsessed with security: they partly embrace and partly make manifest communities of values and attitudes as well as defense needs. These latter claims need careful analysis because by 2006 the idea of overlapping values and attitudes was being challenged seriously. Robert Kagan has caricatured Americans and Europeans respectively as Martians and Venusians.[1] Emmanuel Todd agrees with Kagan that there are profound differences between the United States and Europe (and he includes the British albeit somewhat ambivalently in this), although he holds a different perspective which includes claims that U.S. power is in precipitous decline.[2] Ex-German Chancellor Gerhard Schröder believes that NATO is "no longer the primary venue where transatlantic partners discuss and coordinate strategies."[3] The gap between defense expenditure on each side of the Atlantic has rapidly widened, 3.9 percent of the gross domestic product (GDP) in the United States and an average of 1.75 percent in Europe. There are massive discrepancies in military capabilities, while France and the United States in particular have major arguments over strategic doctrine, as well as the status of NATO and the CESDP. Finally, in 2003 U.S. Defense Secretary Donald Rumsfeld seemed to completely discount even the value of the Anglo-American special relationship when he declared that the United States could very well do without British troops for the war of liberation in Iraq.[4]

So where does the answer lie concerning questions on the future of U.S.-European relations? Is it to be found in a reformulation of security needs resonating with realist assumptions, or does it lie in a reforging of a community of shared values and attitudes reinforced by appropriate institutions, or is there some kind of third way a la Blair, or should the relationship be terminated and arrangements made for the wake?

NOTHING'S NEW?

Problems that now afflict transatlantic relations are not particularly new, though this issue will be revisited again in the conclusion. However, whether they are new or not, there are no easy answers, and this is no different than in the past. The solution to the current problems cannot be provided by a cold calculation of realist security needs, nor does the answer lie solely in invoking a community of values and attitudes. The problem is that some transatlantic security needs are shared, some are not; and on either side of the Atlantic, attitudes wax, wane, and shift as one would expect in pluralistic societies. Some values which are not shared have a tendency to raise conflict, or at least important challenges for reconciliation: both the Suez Crisis and the Cuban Missile Crisis demonstrated that NATO's Article 5 three musketeers' principle of all-for-one and one-for-all could be overridden by narrower national interests. Similarly, some values and attitudes are shared and some are not; again, those that are not may tend to cause friction and conflict unless managed and controlled carefully. Values and attitudes lack homogeneity as well on both sides of the Atlantic. Nothing is given and nothing can be taken for granted, except that they challenge political leaders to deal with them, and it is how they are dealt with that counts. The idea that shared values and attitudes create a community which can work together harmoniously to perpetuate itself is as fatuous as the hopes at the start of the 20th century that shared values and attitudes and economic interdependence had made war between the European nation-states an impossibility. Apart from other considerations, values can dramatically change as Nazi Germany demonstrated to the cost of all. Also, common values and attitudes are impotent unless there is a political will and the skill to employ them in common enterprises. Bearing these observations in mind, what light might be cast on current problems by the workings of the Anglo-American special relationship and Tony Blair's recent diplomacy?

THE ANGLO-AMERICAN SPECIAL RELATIONSHIP:
A POSSIBLE MODEL?

A close Anglo-American security relationship has been maintained since the 1930s. It continues today, providing an important bridge between the United States and Europe. For example, the July 2004 British Defence Command Paper made it very clear that interoperability with the United States and tasks defined in a manner very similar to the U.S. 2002 strategy document were at the heart of things. Among some of the key points are that the new policy should "enhance our ability to lead or be the framework nation for European (and other coalition) operations where the United States is not engaged." However, there also is an assumption "that the most complex large-scale operations will only be conducted as part of a U.S.-led coalition."[5] This is what might be called the structure for the formal special defense relationship. It also involves intelligence cooperation on a vast scale that stretches back to World War II and the UK-U.S. signals intelligence agreement of 1948.[6] The recent revelations about intelligence-gathering prior to the invasion of Iraq in 2003 provided further evidence of just how extensive this cooperation is. For example, an American representative often sits in on meetings of the UK Joint Intelligence Committee. Britain and the United States operate so closely in the intelligence sphere that it is difficult to see how they can be disentangled.

Nuclear cooperation, most notably with the U.S. supply of delivery vehicles for the UK nuclear deterrent, was made possible by the 1958 U.S.-UK Mutual Defence Agreement, which was renewed in 2004, thus giving Britain the option of purchasing yet another generation of delivery systems from the United States. Part of Britain's contribution to all this is to provide facilities for information-gathering and early radar warning for the U.S. national missile defense program, most notably at Fylingdales and Menwith Hill. Buttressing the formal is a long-standing informal special defense relationship. During the Falklands War of 1982, the U.S. Navy dramatically increased its logistical and intelligence support of the Royal Navy without any formal agreement having to be made. As the U.S. Navy Secretary later commented, this was illustrative of a relationship like no other between foreign navies.[7] More recently, the relationship between the U.S. Air Force (USAF) and the Royal Air Force (RAF) has been described as "an excellent model of successful coalition relations," with the further observations that personnel "exchange tours have long been a staple of the relationship" and that the RAF "has continued to fly (since the end of the Cold War) with U.S. airmen and provide U.S. access to bases in the United Kingdom, Cyprus, and Diego Garcia during Operation ENDURING FREEDOM in Afghanistan and Operation IRAQI FREEDOM."[8] This informal special relationship often can bond tighter than formal arrangements.

Britain consistently has struggled to establish a robust and permanent transatlantic alliance. It stretches back to Winston Churchill's three spheres strategy for British foreign policy — the Commonwealth, the United States, and Europe. It was at the heart of Ernest Bevin's strategy for dealing with both the danger of revanchism in West Germany and the threat from Moscow. In 1979 British Foreign Secretary David Owen wrote: "I see no incompatibility whatever in maintaining a strong commitment to the Atlantic Alliance with Community membership and full participation in the responsibilities of Commonwealth."[9] And in 1999 Blair declared his aim of establishing Britain as "a pivotal power, as a power that is at the crux of alliances and international politics which shape the world and its future."[10] Britain would play, among other things, a pivotal role between the United States and Europe, with Blair trying to mediate between them and hold things together. But this is not simple. The Anglo-American special relationship could hardly be held forth as a model for Europe to emulate if Britain is seen as Washington's poodle. Dispelling such an image often can be difficult. For example, the British triumph over U.S. negotiators in the 1976-77 Bermuda 2 Air Services Agreement and Britain's upholding of its favored position ever since is not exactly likely to have the same impact as the image of the British poodle; actually, a picture of a bulldog savaging the American bald eagle would depict a more accurate aspect of the relationship in this important commercial sphere.[11]

But there are other problems as well. Britain does have conflicting loyalties. Its vision of Europe, particularly of a European security role, is more compatible with American views than those of any of its European partners; consequently, it clashes with the visions of other leading member states, most notably with France's. Europe is not homogeneous in its view of the United States by any means, but it is probably true to say that France represents the most challenging European position for the United States and for the continuation of a strong transatlantic security arrangement. France is determined to develop a strong European independent defense capability and to throw off the shackles of what it sees as U.S. hegemonic dominance. For its part, the United States in the security sphere has three clear priorities: it wants Europe to shoulder more of the burden of defense and increase its military capabilities; it wants NATO to remain the dominant defense organization for Europe and the Atlantic region and to develop out-of-area capabilities; and it wants an official presence at the EU table to bring pressures to bear and to ensure that the EU does not become too independent-minded in security matters. These positions represent substantial challenges for those who want to perpetuate and strengthen the transatlantic alliance. Matters have not been made any easier by the values and policies of the administration of George W. Bush, for example, its penchant for unilateralism, its insistence on the universalism of American democratic and free-market values, and its strategy of preventative strike.

BLAIR'S PIVOTING

The idea that Britain might act in such a way as to reconcile and bring together Europe and the United States in a special kind of relationship is not as far-fetched as one might think. While an important part of the thesis here is that there is an Anglo-American special relationship that might provide a model for future transatlantic developments, it also is contended that a high degree of specialness has existed between the United States and Europe as a whole since the 1940s. The suggestion, therefore, is not that Blair and his successors might conjure something up from nothing, or indeed that Britain could in some way consummate this project alone. Germany has had a long-standing close relationship with the United States, and the Schröder breach may very well be an aberration rather than a new trend. Also, many countries in eastern and central Europe, most notably Poland, have strong ethnic and political ties and sympathies with the United States. Bearing these points in mind, let us turn to the CESDP to see how Blair's pivotal role has performed in recent years.

Suggestions of developing an independent European military capability have met repeatedly with muted and sometimes not so muted criticisms from the United States. During Clinton's time, these took the form of Ambassador Dobbins' demarche and Madeleine Albright's warnings of prospective problems for NATO; during George W. Bush's time, we have had Donald Rumsfeld's characteristically robust warnings about reducing the effectiveness of NATO and disturbing transatlantic links. With the St. Malo rapprochement between Blair and Chirac in 1998 and the launch of the CESDP, Blair was confronted with a delicate balancing act. American warnings of undermining NATO as well as the overall transatlantic relationship rang in one ear and Chirac's obviously different interpretation of the CESDP rang in the other. Chirac: "There cannot be a Europe without its own defense system."[12] Between 1998 and 2006, there were developments in the CESDP, and Blair has managed to tread the tightrope. This has not been achieved without serious wobbling by Blair on that tightrope. Sometimes the unbalancing came from the United States, sometimes it came from Europe. At their first meeting in late February 2001, Blair extracted agreement from Bush and his advisers that they would support the European Defence Initiative launched at St. Malo, providing it did not compromise NATO, in return for UK support, albeit muted, for the U.S. National Missile Defense System and agreement to allow the United States to upgrade its facilities at Fylingdales as part of that program.[13] However, things did not develop smoothly. The championing by the United States in 2002 of a NATO Reaction Force (RF) rather stole the thunder from Europe's proposal for a Rapid Reaction Force, which at that time was languishing in "planning stages" largely on paper. Europe — pushed on by Britain and France — firmed up commitments inter alia to develop 13 battle groups of 1,500 troops each, deployable within 30 days. The European Defence Agency also has been created to promote harmonization of equipment, research and development policy, and common European procurement policies.

At the same time there have been these positive developments, Britain has managed to head off suggestions that would have run counter to the interests of NATO and the United States. The European military policy planning cell agreed on in 2003 has thus been embedded in Supreme Headquarters Allied Powers Europe (SHAPE), developments with the Western European Union (WEU) have been blocked, and provisions have been excluded from the now defunct European Constitution which ran contrary to upholding the status of NATO. At the same time, there have been developments in NATO, strongly backed by the UK, which speak to American desires for its new agenda. Out-of-area operations are proliferating, and the expansion of NATO has provided forward positions for the United States in its posture vis-à-vis the Middle East and oil-rich and strategically placed central Asian republics. These republics are strategically placed not only for oil, of course, but also in the confrontation with terrorism. As Luca Ratti explains from the realist perspective:

> The United States has continued to use NATO as a political mechanism to secure adherence to its strategic and foreign policy objectives, forestall the development of an independent European security and defence structure, and acquire strategic advantages useful for the projection of U.S. power towards Central Asia, the Middle East, and the Caucasus. The alliance's main undertakings since the end of the Cold War, such as intervention in the Balkans, expansion to former Warsaw Pact states, political co-existence with Russia, and, more recently, the handing over of peacekeeping responsibilities in Bosnia and Macedonia to the European Union are profoundly intertwined with U.S. strategic interests.[14]

One should add that they also are intertwined with Europe's as well.

CONCLUSION

Senior scholars such as Geir Lundestad and Georges-Henri Soutou may be right in claiming that aspects of the current transatlantic difficulties are so corrosive that they differ from those that have afflicted the alliance in the past, that there will be further transatlantic drift, and that France and the United States are irreconcilable.[15] It is true that the Cold War has passed, there has been a resurgence of U.S. unilateralism, and significant changes have taken place in Europe, not to mention the recent dominance of a rigid neo-conservative ideology in the United States. Still, one wonders whether these developments are any more significant than the Suez Crisis, European integration from the 1950s to the 1990s, or the unilateralism made manifest in U.S. policies such as Nixon's New Economic Policy and the waging of a war in Vietnam. Thus, despite all the difficulties that have buffeted the NATO Alliance and transatlantic relations generally over the last decade or so, one should neither see them as something new, nor ignore the progress that has been made towards smoothing things out and strengthening ties. NATO has developed since the end of the Cold War and now provides new security pay-offs for all its members: stability and anchorage for the ex-communist states in a democratic Europe buttressed by the expansion of the EU; a powerful voice in world affairs — often forgotten is that the only time Article 5's all-for-one and one-for-all principle has been invoked was to help the United States in the aftermath of 9/11; NATO now conducts out-of-area operations that are quite significant security-wise; and NATO expansion has enhanced the alliance's posture with regard to strategically sensitive areas, i.e., the Middle East, the Caucasus, and Central Asia. At the same time CESDP has developed modestly and in a way that is largely acceptable to the United States and which has encouraged Europe. No matter how hell-bent the French might be on developing an independent European military capability, they know that it would not be credible without British participation; that requires some compromise and shift in French policies, both of which having been in evidence in recent years. As for the community of values and attitudes, while these remain badly bruised by 9/11's aftermath and differences over environmental, social, and economic policies, there also is a growing awareness of the importance of transatlantic ties, with both sides having taken steps to try to improve things, following Blair in the vanguard.

This picture is not as promising as the rather over-optimistic scenario painted by Timothy Garton Ash, although some of the evidence he cites for the mutual economic benefits to be derived by both sides is persuasive: each has over $3 trillion of assets in the other.[16] The picture merely emphasizes that an important political game needs to be played and decisions taken to negotiate what undoubtedly will be a difficult way forward. One route, which may not be too fanciful, is that instead of Britain ditching the special relationship for the sake of its role in Europe, Blair should continue with his pivotal role and attempt to renew and widen the special relationship that has bound the United States and Europe so closely together since 1945. In the field of security, he has already marked up some successes by obtaining compromises with France and rather grudging acceptance of them by the United States. One thing certain is that the relationship between the United States and Europe cannot be encapsulated by either realist security prescriptions or by liberal conceptions of moral and attitudinal communities. There is no clear-cut dichotomy between interests and affections: interests often are determined by affections and vice versa. If Europe and the United States are to move ahead together in an ever closer union, then policies that reflect common affections and interests must have pride of place and must be cultivated in order to allow tolerance of differences of interests and affections on both sides. Moreover, political decisions will need to be taken to exploit these possibilities in the same way that both American and British politicians, notwithstanding differences, difficulties, and clashes of interest, have taken decisions which have kept alive a special Anglo-American relationship for well over half a century.

ENDNOTES

1. Robert Kagan, *Of Paradise and Power: America and Europe in the New World Order*, New York: Knopf, 2003.

2. Emmanuel Todd, *After the Empire: The Breakdown of American Order*, London: Constable, 2004.

3. Gerhard Schröder at the 41st Munich Conference on Security Policy on February 12, 2005, *www.druckversion.studien-von-zeitfragen.net/Speech perecent20Ch perecent20Schroeder perecent2041th perecent20Munich perecent20Conference.pdf*.

4. "Germany Urges NATO Reform and Re-think of Transatlantic Ties," Agence France Press, February 13, 2005; for defence expenditure figures, see S. Marsh and H. Mackenstein, *The International Relations of the European Union*, Harlow, United Kingdom: Pearson, 2005, p. 91.

5. "Delivering Security in a Changing World: Future Capabilities," British Defence Command Paper 6269, July 2004.

6. Jeffrey T. Richelson, *The Ties That Bind: Intelligence Cooperation Between UK/USA Countries*, London: Routledge, 1990 (revised edition).

7. David Dimbleby and David Reynolds, *An Ocean Apart: The Relationship Between Britain and America in the Twentieth Century*, London: Hodder and Staughton, 1988, pp. 314-315.

8. Christopher Finn and Paul D. Berg, "Anglo-American Strategic Air Power Co-operation in the Cold War and Beyond," *Air and Space Power Journal*, Winter 2004.

9. David Owen, "Britain and the United States," in W. E. Leuchtenburg *et al., Britain and the United States: Four Views to Mark the Silver Jubilee*, London: Heinemann, 1979, p. 76.

10. Blair's speech at the Lord Mayor's Banquet, London, November 22, 1999, *www.the-islander.org.ac/oldsite/1461.htm*.

11. Alan P. Dobson, "Regulation or Competition: Negotiating the Anglo-American Air Service Agreement 1977," *Journal of Transport History*, Vol. 2, 1994, pp. 144-165.

12. "EU Defence Plan Baffles NATO," December 3, 2003, *www.news.bbc.co.uk/1/hi/world/europe3287009.stm*.

13. Anthony Seldon *et al.*, *Blair*, London: Free Press, 2005, p. 612.

14. Luca Ratti, "Post-Cold War NATO and International Relations Theory: The Case for Neo-Classical Realism," forthcoming in *Journal of Transatlantic Studies*, Vol. 4, No.1, Spring 2006.

15. Geir Lundestad, "Towards Atlantic Drift," and Georges-Henri Soutou, "Three Rifts, Two Reconciliations: Franco-American Relations during the Fifth Republic," David M. Andrews, ed., *The Atlantic Alliance Under Stress: U.S.-European Relations After Iraq*, Cambridge, Cambridge University Press, 2005, pp. 9-30, 102-128.

16. Timothy Garton Ash, *Free World*, London: Penguin, 2004.

HOW TO AVOID A TRANSATLANTIC RIFT OVER IRAN[1]

Dr. Guillaume Parmentier

Originally appeared in *Financial Times*, April 28, 2006. Reprinted with permission.

A painful conclusion must be drawn from the Iran controversy: Two Gulf wars have taught Middle Eastern rulers — and to a large extent their populations — that if Iraq had possessed nuclear weapons, Saddam Hussein would probably still be in power. The United States and the international coalition would not have dared attack him when he invaded Kuwait.

There can be little doubt that most Iranians support their leaders' nuclear plans. Iran sees itself, somewhat justifiably, as a great nation surrounded by potential enemies in an unstable region. The Arabs never liked the Persians. The Sunnis hate the Shias, who predominate in Iran. Israel and Pakistan have nuclear weapons. The U.S. military is next door in Iraq, and President George W. Bush has labelled Iran part of the "Axis of Evil."

All western countries agree that the problem is very grave. If Iran tests a weapon, other regional powers will follow. This does not mean the United States and Europe will always see eye to eye on the issue. The Americans and Europeans have different perspectives. For the United States, the regime is the problem. Since September 11, 2001 (9/11), America feels that the main danger to international security comes from governments that combine hostility towards U.S. policy with poor human rights records. For the Europeans, the issue is essentially one of nuclear proliferation, necessitating that attention therefore be paid to the regional equation, since this is the main catalyst for a national decision to obtain nuclear weapons. On that basis, a serious transatlantic crisis may be in the making if the western powers do not reconcile their divergent perspectives.

For the Europeans, it is wrong to concentrate exclusively on the nuclear issue. The broader problem lies in Iran's relationship with the rest of the world. Many Iranians, especially young ones, want more information, contacts, and ideas from abroad. Mahmoud

Ahmadi-Nejad's victory in the 2005 presidential elections can be attributed to a rejection of a corrupt elite rather than support for his reactionary views. A more open Iran would make it difficult for the mullahs to impose their orthodoxy, which bears heavily on the lives of Iranians in ways that most of them resent. This does not mean Iranians want to become western, or are "pro-American," or that a U.S. military strike and/or international economic sanctions would not be condemned universally in Iran. But, as Zbigniew Brzezinski, the former U.S. national security adviser, wrote recently: "The mullahs are Iran's past, not its future." Western interest lies in Iran becoming more open to the rest of the world.

Unfortunately, it will be difficult to open Iran. The United States officially does not recognize the country, although there have recently been informal and discreet talks with Iran on Iraq. The contacts essentially have to come from Europe.

Even more difficult, Iran's leaders understand the population's desire to connect to the world, and they fear for their control over the people. No doubt this is what lies behind the recent and revolting radicalization of the language used by Mr Ahmadi-Nejad and other Iranian leaders: the anti-Semitic slurs, the threats against Israel, and the denial of the Holocaust make it almost impossible for the West to extend an open hand to Iran. It is therefore difficult for the Europeans to continue to maintain a dialogue on the model of the now-shelved EU3 effort on uranium enrichment. This places them in a difficult position because they can no longer come forward with clear policy options: while they do not disagree with the U.S. diagnosis, they remain convinced that fixes will not work. The U.S. refusal last year to offer security guarantees and diplomatic recognition as a complement to the EU3 approach has deprived Europe of its main tool. Western options remain drastically limited. It would be wise to recognize this limitation and avoid definitive statements that cannot be backed by action.

Although Iran's government is unpopular, Europeans recognize that the post-1979 regime is the country's first genuinely national one for a long time: the Shah was perceived widely by Iranians as an American puppet, and previous regimes also had been foreign-dominated. Foreign interference in Iranian affairs always will be strongly resented. The West must keep this in mind when dealing with Iran to avoid cementing popular support for the leadership. Talk of military strikes, denied for the present by Mr. Bush, is exceedingly unhelpful in this respect. The analogy with Iraq is wrong, at least at this stage. If only for military reasons, occupation and regime change are out of the question. "Selective strikes" against nuclear installations would only ensure the eventual development by Iran of nuclear weapons, with massive popular support. And isolating Iran would only buttress an unpopular regime and give it a scapegoat to blame for the country's difficulties. Any embargo that would strike the population would be as counterproductive as has been the U.S. embargo on Cuba.

Better to hold our nose and maintain contact with the country, while using information, visits, economic relations, and the like in the hope that it will weaken the leadership in the long haul. After all, it worked with the Soviets.

ENDNOTE

1. This article, which appeared in the *Financial Times* on April 28, 2006, is available at *news.ft.com/cms/s/07e2d53c-d615-11da8b3a-0000779e2340.html*.

Two documents are provided here. The first, by Colonel Randall Larsen, summarizes key issues that emerged from two simulated bioterrorist attacks, Dark Winter and Atlantic Storm. The second piece, by Dr. Daniel Hamilton and Dr. Bradley Smith, examines the lessons of Atlantic Storm in greater depth.

DARK WINTER/ATLANTIC STORM: KEY ISSUES FROM TWO EXECUTIVE LEVEL EXERCISES

Colonel Randall J. Larsen

Background.

On June 22-23, 2001, the Johns Hopkins Center for Civilian Biodefense Strategies, in collaboration with the Center for Strategic and International Studies, the Analytic Services Institute for Homeland Security, and the Oklahoma National Memorial Institute for the Prevention of Terrorism, held a senior-level exercise called Dark Winter. It simulated a covert smallpox attack on the United States. The first such exercise of its kind, Dark Winter was conceived to examine the challenges that senior-level policymakers would have to deal with if confronted by a bioterrorist attack initiating outbreaks of a contagious disease. The exercise was intended to increase awareness among senior national security experts of the scope and character of the threat posed by biological weapons, and to bring about actions that would improve prevention and response strategies. Participants included the Governor of Oklahoma, a former U.S. Senator, a former advisor to four U.S. Presidents, the former Director of the Federal Bureau of Investigation, the former Director of the Central Intelligence Agency, the former Deputy Secretary of Defense, the former Assistant Secretary for Health and Human Services for Emergency Planning, and other national security experts.

Key Issues.

Many of the key issues identified in this domestically-focused exercise also emerged as critical issues in the internationally-focused Atlantic Storm exercise conducted on January 14, 2005. (See Atlantic Storm article by Dr. Dan Hamilton below.)

Key issues from Dark Winter also explored during Atlantic Storm were:

1. Epidemics and pandemics, whether natural or man-made, do not recognize state or international boundaries. However, most response mechanisms are based on state organizations and leaders (Dark Winter) and national organizations and leaders (Atlantic Storm). The only effective response mechanisms will be those that utilize multijurisdictional/international planning and response.

2. Leaders at all levels will face difficult decisions due to limited resources. Who will receive the vaccines and treatments? Is it best to share supplies in an attempt to stop the spread before it reaches one's own state/country? Who should enjoy priority in receiving these lifesaving drugs: medical and public health personnel, government leaders, children, law enforcement, military, elderly, etc.? Such priorities must be considered and resolved prior to a crisis.

3. In addition to the obvious public health aspects of an epidemic/pandemic (in these two exercises, it was smallpox; however, most contagious pathogens would present the same challenges), the resulting economic catastrophe could far surpass the public health implications in terms of adverse effects on national security. In 2003, severe acute respiratory syndrome (SARS) killed only 800 people worldwide, yet caused enormous economic disruptions throughout Asia and in Canada. Often, the damage to the economy can be attributed to fear (SARS), but in other cases, it is caused by the draconian reactions by government leaders. Leaders must walk that fine line between publicly minimizing the scale of the threat, which otherwise leads to a loss of trust from the public and uncontrolled fear (well-documented in the 1918 flu pandemic) on one hand, and over-reacting (Swine flu 1972—where more people died from the hastily prepared vaccine than from the flu itself), on the other.

4. Travel restrictions and quarantine are other issues explored during Dark Winter and Atlantic Storm. Not only do these measures

pose their own unique challenges, but they may not be the best solution to halting the spread of a pandemic. From an economic stand point, a global economy based on just-in-time delivery would shut down if faced with severe travel restrictions. Additionally, many medical experts believe these actions would be of limited benefit to public health, but would cause a great drain on resources which could be used for more important services. As just one example, the personnel necessary to enforce a quarantine could be employed instead to ensure the rapid and efficient distribution of key supplies.

Conclusion.

The bottom line is that leaders must reach out across jurisdictional lines, both interstate and international, to prepare properly for large-scale public health disasters. This is not the sort of activity that can be developed and executed properly on the fly. It must come from plans and exercises that were well-tested prior to the crisis. Epidemics and pandemics do not recognize state and international borders. Planning and response programs based on 20th-century attitudes about borders will fail when faced with 21st-century public health challenges.

ATLANTIC STORM:
FACING THE BIOTERROR CHALLENGE

Dr. Daniel S. Hamilton
and
Dr. Bradley T. Smith

In early 2005, 11 former ministers and heads of government from Europe and North America confronted a simulated threat no one should ever have to face in the real world: The use of contagious disease as a weapon. Our simulation, Atlantic Storm, was designed to provoke the imagination and to prompt action by making the reality of deliberate epidemics more vivid and by underscoring our shared responsibility to prevent this eventuality if possible, and also to prepare for and respond to such a threat at the international level. The lessons learned from the Atlantic Storm scenario are relevant to all large-scale, destabilizing epidemics of infectious disease — be they natural or intentional. Atlantic Storm illustrated that preparedness matters — leaders cannot be expected to create the necessary systems to respond to an epidemic in the midst of an international security crisis. With the looming threat of a global influenza pandemic, there is even more urgency to reinforce international health security.

Background.

Atlantic Storm was a ministerial-level exercise simulating a series of bioterrorism attacks on the transatlantic community. The exercise occurred on January 14, 2005, in Washington, DC. It was designed, organized, and convened by a team from the Center for Biosecurity of the University of Pittsburgh Medical Center (*www. upmc-biosecurity.org*), the Center for Transatlantic Relations at the Paul H. Nitze School of Advanced International Studies of Johns Hopkins University (*transatlantic.sais-jhu.edu*), and the Transatlantic Biosecurity Network.

Summit principals, who were all current or former senior government leaders, were challenged to address strategic issues such as attaining situational awareness in the wake of a bioattack, coping with scarcity of critical medical resources such as vaccine, deciding how to manage the movement of people across borders, and communicating with their publics. Atlantic Storm illustrated that much might be done in advance to minimize illness and death as well as the social, economic, and political disruption that could be caused by a bioterror attack or international epidemic.

Any lessons to be harvested are welcome at this time, especially given growing concerns about the possibility of an avian influenza pandemic that would require an international response. However, international leaders cannot create the necessary response systems in the midst of a crisis. Medical, public health, security, diplomatic, and emergency response systems, as well as critical resources such as medicines and vaccines, must be in place before a bioattack occurs or a pandemic emerges.

The Atlantic Storm scenario was centered around a campaign of fictitious deliberate outbreaks of smallpox in Europe and North America. The organizers used the best available medical and epidemiological data on smallpox to design a conservative version of the outbreak to be used to drive the exercise. The primary goal of Atlantic Storm was not to "model" a smallpox outbreak, but rather to illuminate strategic challenges to be faced by the international community in responding collectively to a bioterrorist attack or any other large-scale epidemic. A number of diseases could have been chosen to drive the exercise. A document explaining all assumptions and scenario design decisions is available on the Atlantic Storm website (*www.atlantic-storm.org*).

What to do?

The Atlantic Storm scenario—destructive and disruptive as it was—could have been much worse. Unless we forge new health security alliances to meet the bioterrorist threat, an attack of mass lethality is not a matter of whether, but when. Just as Atlantic Storm began, the scientific journal *Nature* announced the development of biological techniques that permit rapid, accurate synthesis of long segments of DNA from nonliving parts, and in October 2005 the 1918 "Spanish" flu virus was re-created in the laboratory. These and other developments will help researchers seeking new medicines and vaccines. But they also put the synthesis (and therefore the modification) of large viruses such as smallpox, and perhaps even bacteria, within the reach of hundreds of laboratories around the world. The age of engineered biological weapons is here. It is not science fiction.

There is evidence that nonstate actors are actively seeking to develop biological weapons and will not refrain from using them. Can we shift the advantage from such potential mass murderers? Absolutely. But it requires the will and the imagination to take corrective actions that are more than piecemeal extensions of current policies. Following are several concrete recommendations.

- The international community must plan for coordinated responses to major bioattacks and epidemics. Such plans should include strategic and operational details commensurate with that conducted by major international security organizations for more traditional threats. The roles and relevance of such organizations also should be reviewed in the light of such threats.

The first step is to recognize that this threat requires something more holistic than buying more vaccine or training more doctors. It means integrating our public health and national security communities in ways that allow us to supplement our traditional security emphasis on territorial defense with a focus on integration and cooperation across borders. Werner Hoyer, member of the German Bundestag and former Deputy Foreign Minister, who played the German Chancellor in Atlantic Storm, stated after conclusion of the exercise: "For someone who has been around in the security and defense fields in its traditional sense for many years, this was quite a surprising and breathtaking exercise. . . . This is something I think a very small minority of politicians in Europe are aware of. . . ."

Many of the senior participants in Atlantic Storm concluded that key multilateral frameworks such as the North Atlantic Treaty Organization (NATO) and the European Union (EU) are limited in their ability to cope with the unique challenges posed by a bioweapon-induced spread of epidemic disease. Would a bioweapon attack that threatens a nation's health rather than its territory warrant a collective response under NATO's mutual defense clause or the EU's "solidarity clause"? What might such a response entail, and is either institution equipped for such action? In Atlantic Storm, the relevance of a traditional security organization such as NATO to new types of health security threats was raised when Turkey called on NATO to invoke its Article 5 mutual defense clause and for NATO nations to provide vaccine to help the nation respond to the simulated outbreak in Istanbul. The Prime Minister of Italy, played in Atlantic Storm by Stefano Silvestri, responded to this request from Turkey in the following words:

> I can understand why Turkey has asked for the activation of Article 5 of NATO, Turkey not being yet inside [the] European Union. . . . The problem, of course, is that it is not necessarily a military response that we should give. We should give a political response to Turkey, for the moment.

However, despite the view expressed by Mr. Silvestri, joint planning for traditional international security contingencies has occurred in NATO and other security alliances for decades. Planning with that degree of rigor and strategic and operational detail, but now for international response to epidemics, is definitely needed to cope with potential biothreats of international consequence.

Transatlantic cooperation also is often the core of effective nonproliferation work, such as the Cooperative Threat Reduction Program, EU-Russia programs, or the G8 Global Partnership. However, biosecurity efforts often have remained orphans of such programs; they must now be given high priority and resources commensurate to the challenge.

According to Jan Eliasson, President of the UN General Assembly and former Swedish Ambassador to the United States, who played the Swedish Prime Minister in Atlantic Storm: "We live in a time of new threats. . . . What we now see is that health and security go together, so we have to combine them, and I think the lesson we should draw from this . . . is that we don't have the organizational structures to deal with the new threats."

More effective international planning also means achieving greater consensus on the science behind such efforts. In Atlantic Storm, participants were stunned to realize that many problems they had assumed would be resolved by straightforward scientific research were, in fact, complicated issues about which scientists from different countries and organizations disagreed. To resolve these issues, therefore, political decisions would ultimately need to be made.

The Prime Minister of Poland, played in Atlantic Storm by the former Prime Minister of Poland, Jerzy Buzek, made this point very clear in the context of proposed vaccine dilution: "Scientists have different opinions, and we must make a political decision on this. . . ."

- Nations should not only strengthen their own national plans to respond to biothreats, they should ensure that such plans are coordinated with those of neighbors and major partners.

There is little mutual understanding among nations. For example, Atlantic Storm participants were surprised by the wide differences in national smallpox vaccine stockpiles. Some countries had enough for all their citizens, while others only had enough for 1 percent or even less. A former Dutch Interior Minister, who played the role of the Dutch Prime Minister during Atlantic Storm, stated: "When I saw the list [of vaccine stocks], that was a shock to me, how little prepared many countries are, even rich Western countries, to address this kind of problem."

There are no accepted benchmarks to judge a country's ability to handle the array of potential biothreats, but some countries have made major investments and some have made none. What *Atlantic Storm* illustrated — as do many real-world biosecurity crises such as severe acute respiratory syndrome (SARS) or an influenza pandemic — is that it is in the explicit interests of the United States and other countries to ensure as few "weak links" as possible in the international community's ability to mount an effective public health response. Health issues have become integral elements of national security. Developed countries are only as secure as the world's weakest public health system. Moreover, their own health systems are largely unprepared for an intentional attack using infectious disease.

- The United States should work with the international community to augment greatly the capacity of the World Health Organization (WHO) to respond to the health and medical consequences of biological attacks or pandemics.

In Atlantic Storm, leaders turned to WHO. Yet it is woefully underfunded and understaffed. As Gro Harlem Brundtland, former director general of WHO, commented during the exercise, that organization "is like a middle-sized hospital in England in total resources." The scientists and health officials of WHO are highly capable, dedicated, and hard-working. But Atlantic Storm showed that even experienced politicians have unrealistic notions of what WHO would be able to deliver in a crisis, given its current budgetary, political, and organizational limits. Mr. Brundtland thus went on to conclude: "If leaders at this level are realizing that you have a crisis and that you need the WHO to be doing important roles, they also will [have to] support, with extra budgetary resources, what's necessary."

The 2004-05 WHO budget for bioterrorism preparedness is estimated to be only $6.3 million. The entire 2004-05 WHO biennial budget is $2.8 billion, 70 percent of which comes from voluntary donations made by nations, international organizations, nongovernment organizations (NGOs), and private philanthropies. This is an impossible situation for an organization that must have the flexibility to respond rapidly to emerging epidemics, and raises questions about WHO's capacity to respond to large disease epidemics in multiple locations around the world. The new International Health Regulations, approved in early 2005, may help bolster WHO's clout internationally, but resources still will be severely limited.

Moreover, some issues cannot be addressed even by a stronger WHO. During a global outbreak, for example, who would decide which countries should receive scarce vaccines or medicines? This is a life-or-death political decision—a "tragic choice"—that is beyond the brief of any international organization. During Atlantic Storm, principals hoped that WHO could serve as an independent "honest broker" for such politically sensitive decisions. In reality, such decisions are likely to be made only by the national leaders who control these scarce medical resources. The challenges facing international coordination of scarce medical resources are illustrated by the reality that EU nations have decided against a shared stockpile of smallpox vaccine because of this very issue—the difficulty of allocating scarce vaccine to multiple member states in an emergency.

If EU nations—nations that are so closely aligned that most share the same currency—have been unable to agree on how to share a security asset as critical as smallpox vaccine, the prospects for broader international sharing mechanisms appear bleak indeed.

- The very real prospect of bioterrorism requires new approaches, not only by doctors, scientists, and health care authorities, but by national security communities as well.

Traditional concepts of deterrence and dissuasion must be tailored to the threat of asymmetric warfare by state or nonstate actors. Deterrence is unlikely to play the same role in managing the asymmetric bioweapons threat that it played in managing the apocalyptic Soviet threat. Dissuasion can be an effective complement to deterrence. Whereas deterrence focuses on stopping identifiable adversaries from employing real capabilities, dissuasion aims at stopping potential adversaries from ever developing such capabilities. Dissuasion could become an important new link in national security strategy by covering the grey zone between providing assurance to publics and partners, and deterring adversaries. In the early days of the Cold War, deterrence was a rather hazy concept. Once equipped with a full-fledged strategic theory, it acquired a role of central importance. The same may hold true for the concept of dissuasion today—but only if it, too, is equipped with the full set of analyses and calculations needed to bring it to life.

These concepts require not only the trust of other partners, but also their active cooperation, which means they must be embedded in new diplomatic approaches. For instance, how should arms control treaties geared to states be adapted to nonstate actors? The global legal regime focuses on the activities of states, not subnational groups or individuals. It is weak with regard to monitoring and verification, and often fails to deal adequately with the significant differences between the types of weapons often lumped together under the term "weapons of mass destruction" (WMD). On the other hand, recent decades offer clear examples of successful diplomacy regarding nuclear weapons—Belarus, Kazakhstan, Ukraine, Argentina, Brazil, and South Africa were all persuaded to abandon their nuclear weapons activities. In earlier decades, Germany, Japan, South Korea, and Turkey also were dissuaded from going nuclear by integration within stable alliances. We need to focus on how such efforts can be adapted to today's more complex challenges.

- The absence of available medical countermeasures (i.e., medicines, vaccines, and diagnostic tests), the inadequacies of health information systems, and the lack of mass distribution systems for medicines and vaccines will limit leaders' capacities to deal with large-scale epidemics. Much more can and should be done now to acquire these resources in order to give international leaders more effective response options when they are faced with a large-scale bioterrorist attack or natural pandemic.

Leaders would be far less inclined to pursue drastic actions if there were ready supplies of vaccine or medicine that could be used to cope with large pandemics—and effective systems to get those countermeasures to the people who need them. But there is currently a critical lack of new medicines and vaccines for all infectious diseases, not just those that could be used as weapons. National and international investments should be directed toward four areas. First, the United States and the international community need to create the capacity to develop and mass produce tens or hundreds of millions of doses of vaccines and medicines on short notice. Atlantic Storm leaders were stunned when they realized that many NATO and EU members—not to mention their poorer neighbors—did not have enough smallpox vaccine for their populations. The lack of sufficient vaccine stocks and the severely limited capacity to produce new vaccine eliminated many of the strategic options that the leaders could have used to respond to the epidemic, thus forcing them to consider measures such as closing borders and large-scale quarantine that could have had severe economic, social, and political repercussions. This lack of vaccine stocks and production capacity is not specific to smallpox; investment in the development of medicine and vaccines for virtually all infectious diseases has been declining for decades, resulting in pipelines that are producing only a trickle of new lifesaving products to counter infectious disease threats.

Stockpiling vaccines and medicines for specific biothreat agents such as smallpox is a good intermediate step. But the real answer is re-creating drug design and manufacture so we can develop whatever is needed on short notice. A comprehensive effort to render nations immune to the mass lethality that can be caused by disease must include an international "rapid reaction" capacity to produce and deliver vaccines and medicines against the plagues that can destabilize economies, disrupt societies, and kill millions.

Second, the United States and the international community should build medical and public health information systems that would provide leaders with enough situational awareness to make decisions and direct resources in response to a bioattack. In Atlantic Storm, leaders were provided with far more situational awareness than they would have had in a real crisis. They were given the locations and numbers of reported smallpox cases in almost real time, and they were constantly updated as information changed. If this had been a real bioattack or epidemic affecting cities in multiple countries, leaders would have had a great deal of trouble obtaining even this level of basic information. This would be true not just for top national leaders, but for political, scientific, and health decisionmakers at all levels of the response system. Additionally, this uncertainty will persist for weeks as the epidemic evolves, which is in contrast to many traditional "lights and sirens" security crises—such as the terrorist attacks of September 11, 2001 (9/11), and others—in which it may take only hours or a few days to understand what has happened on the ground.

In the event of a bioattack, hospitals, health departments, emergency management agencies, local and regional political leaders, and national government agencies in most countries are not organized optimally to communicate with each other about location and number of victims; to request national vaccine, medicine, or equipment assets; or to plan for distribution of key resources. Information technology tools and platforms could be designed to share such information. If these systems are built correctly, they also will improve the routine functioning of hospitals. Given the early international ramifications of a bioattack as was seen in Atlantic Storm, these systems must include appropriate procedures for sharing information between nations.

Third, the United States and the international community need to develop and disseminate as appropriate those rapid point-of-care diagnostic technologies that allow doctors and nurses to identify victims of bioterror attacks easily. There are promising technologies in development, but plans for government investment in such technologies are not clear, and there is no strategic effort yet to drive the costs and simplicity down to a point where hospitals or doctors' offices could begin to use them for both routine and emergency practice.

Fourth, the United States and the international community need to develop the systems necessary to rapidly deliver vaccines and drugs to citizens in the event of a large-scale bioattack or a naturally occurring pandemic. Such systems would mean the difference between a community coping successfully with a crisis and a community whose efforts devolve to fighting over scarce resources. Only a few U.S. cities or states appear to be capable of distributing vital medical resources rapidly in a crisis, and we suspect the same is true in most other nations.

Conclusion.

The world is on the cusp of exponential change in challenges posed by pathogens and their accessibility to state and nonstate actors. These challenges require actions beyond piecemeal extensions of current policies. They require something more holistic than disease-specific stockpiles of medicines or vaccine. It is not just a matter of buying more vaccine or training more doctors. It is a question of how we integrate public health and national security communities in ways that allow us to deal with an unprecedented challenge.

Atlantic Storm showed that even experienced international leaders, when faced with an unfolding epidemic and the resulting uncertainty, would have limited options and stark choices, given the conditions that exist today. Preparation is essential: international leaders cannot be expected to develop the requisite response systems in the midst of a crisis. The exercise made clear that there is much that can be done to improve overall biosecurity for both intentional and natural epidemics—a critical lesson given the growing possibility of an avian influenza pandemic. Transatlantic and international initiatives to enhance biosecurity — the Global Health Security Action Group, the European Commission's Heath Security Committee, the recently announced International Partnership on Avian and Pandemic Influenza—are beginning to gain prominence, but much more work is needed. The nations of the Atlantic Community should lead this effort and include as many partners as possible.

What is needed is a multilayered, comprehensive effort that seeks to render nations essentially immune to mass lethality and other destabilizing effects of the epidemics that would be caused by the most serious biosecurity threats. While no single tool holds the key to success, a variety of approaches could complement and reinforce each other. The core challenge in addressing bioterrorism (as also is true for naturally occurring epidemics) is to control and minimize the devastation of disease, thereby diminishing any reward that could result from pursuit of an intentional attack and the incentive for staging one.

Given the high level of concern in national capitals around the world regarding the avian flu crisis and potential for a human flu pandemic, imagine the impact on international affairs if flu of such menacing potential was being wielded by a thinking enemy. If the transatlantic community regarded biological weapons and the deliberate large-scale epidemics they would bring as one of the most grave and urgent challenges to international security — and if we were to respond with the level of resources and intellectual firepower that the free world brought to defeating Communism — then we could, in our generation, eliminate bioweapons as agents of mass lethality.

Along the way we would, inevitably, also make profound discoveries about pathogenic microbes and the human response to infection which would lead to significant reduction—or even elimination—of the toll of death and suffering caused by naturally occurring infectious disease, which kills 1,500 people every hour and causes half the premature deaths in the developing world.

We can create the capacity to eliminate large epidemics of infectious disease in our lifetimes. We can enhance our security as we enhance our health. But we must first choose to take on this task — the post-9/11 equivalent of putting a man on the moon. It can happen. But it will require imagination, commitment—and leadership.

Additional information on the Atlantic Storm exercise may be found at *www.atlantic-storm.org*.

REFERENCES

Carter, A. "How to Counter WMD." *Foreign Affairs*, Sept/Oct 2004.

Dalgaard-Nielsen, A., and Hamilton, D. S., eds. *Transatlantic Homeland Security* London: Routledge, 2005.

Enserink, M. "Influenza: Crisis Underscores Fragility of Vaccine Production System." *Science*, 2004.

Frey, S. E., *et al.*, "Clinical Responses to Undiluted and Diluted Smallpox Vaccine." *New Englland Journal of Medicine*, April 25, 2002, Vol. 346, No. 17, pp. 1265–1274.

Global Mercury Report available at *www.hc-sc.gc.ca/english/media/issues/global_mercury/index.html*. Accessed August 5, 2005.

Gouvras, G., "Policies in Place Throughout the World: Actions by the European Union." *International Journal of Infectious Diseases*, Vol. 852, 2004, pp. 521–530.

Hamilton, D. S., and O'Toole, T., "Facing Up to the Bioterror Threat." *International Herald Tribune*, January 31, 2005.

Lien, O., et al., *Getting Medicine to Millions in a Public Health Emergency: Can Retailers Play a Role?* Available at *www.upmc-biosecurity.org/misc/medicine/medicine.html*. Accessed August 9, 2005.

Lindstrom, G., "Protecting the European Homeland — The CBR Dimension." EU Institute for Security Studies, July 2004.

Lutes, C., "The Role of Dissuasion in Combating Weapons of Mass Destruction." *Strategic Insights*, Vol. 3, No. 10, 2004. Available at *www.ccc.nps.navy.mil/si*.

National Institutes of Health, "NIAID Study Results Support Diluting Smallpox Vaccine Stockpile to Stretch Supply" (press release). Bethesda, MD, March 28, 2002. Available at *www2.niaid.nih.gov/newsroom/releases/smallpox.htm*. Accessed August 4, 2005.

Ostfield, M. L., "Bioterrorism as a Foreign Policy Issue," *SAIS Review*, Winter-Spring 2004, Vol. 24, No. 1, pp. 131-146.

Petro, J. B., and Relman, D., "Understanding Threats to Scientific Openness." *Science*, December 12, 2003, p. 1898.

Pilat, J. F., "Dissuasion of Terrorists and Other Non-State Actors." *Strategic Insights*, Vol. 3, No. 10, 2004. Available at *www.ccc.nps.navy.mil/si*.

Sagan, S., "Dissuasion and the NPT Regime: Complementary or Contradictory Strategies?" *Strategic Insights*, Vol. 3, No. 10, 2004. Available at *www.ccc.nps. navy.mil/si*.

Smith, B. T., *et al.*, "After-Action Report. "Navigating the Storm: Report and Recommendations from the Atlantic Storm Exercise." *Biosecur Bioterror*, 2005, Vol. 3, No. 3.

Spellberg, B., *et al.* "Trends in Antimicrobial Drug Development: Implications for the Future." *Clinical Infectious Diseases*, Vol. 38, 2004, pp. 1279–1286.

Sundelius, B., and Grönvall, J., "Strategic Dilemmas of Biosecurity in the European Union." *Biosecure Bioterror*, 2004, Vol. 2, No. 1, pp. 17–23.

Talbot, T. R., *et al.* "Vaccination Success Rate and Reaction Profile with Diluted and Undiluted Smallpox Vaccine: A Randomized Controlled Trial. *JAMA*, September 8, 2004, Vol. 292, No. 10, pp. 1205–1212.

Tian J. *et al.*, "Accurate Multiplex Gene Synthesis from Programmable DNA Microchips." *Nature*, December 23, 2004, Vol. 432, pp. 1050-1054.

Trust for America's Health. *Ready or Not: Protecting the Public's Health in the Age of Bioterrorism – 2004*. Washington, DC: Trust for America's Health, 2004. Available at *healthyamericans.org/reports/bioterror04/*. Accessed August 5, 2005.

Tumpey, T. M., *et al.*, "Characterization of the Reconstructed 1918 Spanish Influenza Pandemic Virus." *Science*, October 7, 2005, Vol. 310, No. 5745, pp. 77-80.

AMERICAN REALIGNMENT IN EUROPE

Dr. Johan Lembke

The United States will restructure its forces and base structure in Europe as part of a global base realignment and closure program to better meet the reality of new threats. This will include a shift of bases eastward and the establishment of forward positions in the Black Sea region, in the southern Caucasus, and in Central Asia. At the strategic level, such realignment in Europe demonstrates America's commitment to long-term security and regional stability further east and will increase America's geostrategic flexibility. At the operational level, U.S. realignment could provide attractive basing and training opportunities, and support a shift towards smaller military installations, fewer support facilities and services, a rotational deployment strategy, and an information-age force.

Traditionally, a permanent military presence in Europe, including in Western Europe, has been construed as a political declaration to long-standing allies, including support for German-American relations. An American military presence in Europe represents, according to the traditional view, a continued commitment to its allies and provides a vehicle for direct influence with regard to the European Union (EU). Given such a history, a significant shift eastward could be interpreted as a quest for "coalitions of the willing" rather than a united Atlantic Alliance. On the other hand, such an eastward realignment could be seen as an effort by both the United States and the North Atlantic Treaty Organization (NATO) more broadly to build coalitions outside Western Europe as needed responses to the complexity of security and international engagement in the 21st century. U.S. realignment and the updating or establishment of military installations further east are not being debated intensely among the NATO partners. Rather, eastward alignment is viewed as a rational effort as part of the wider modernization of the alliance. NATO also remains an important vehicle for the United States to maintain some influence in Europe.

The Black Sea Region.

The Black Sea region, which has ancient links to the European mainland, is located geographically at the crossroads of continental Europe, Eurasia and Central Asia, and the Middle East. Moreover, from a historical perspective, the Black Sea region lies astride the junction of the Russian-Orthodox, Ottoman, and Persian Empires, and the great powers in Western Europe. The wider Black Sea region includes all the countries around the Black Sea (Romania, Bulgaria, Ukraine, Russia, Georgia, and Turkey) plus Moldova and the South Caucasus (Armenia, Azerbaijan, and Georgia); and it serves as a gateway to the northern parts of the wider Middle East. The Black Sea region, located as it is along such critical East-West and North-South corridors, has reemerged as an area of vital strategic importance. It represents the new eastern border of the EU, and is arguably not only a relatively coherent geographical region but also is evolving into more of a distinct political regional construct. The strategic importance of the area can only increase as the EU enlarges further to the East. Thus the region is of vital strategic interest to the EU and to the United States as well.

Russia and Turkey have been and remain the predominant regional powers in the Black Sea region. The U.S. interest in the region has been stronger than that demonstrated by the EU. The western and southern shores of the Black Sea region, touching Romania, Bulgaria, and Turkey, represent the eastern and southeastern borders of NATO, a status that will soon apply to the EU as well. Russia still has significant interests in the Black Sea region. The influence and interest of both the EU and the United States from the Adriatic Sea to the Caspian Sea regions have increased and will continue to grow. This broad situation, entailing an enlargement from the Baltic Sea to the western shores of the Black Sea, fosters a geopolitical shift in the Black Sea region. This shift could include new forms of cooperation and competition among external powers, altered relations between regional powers and their relations, in turn, with middle powers, and emerging alliances and relations of countries in the region with external powers. Bulgaria and Romania were among seven countries to join NATO in March 2004. They signed the EU accession treaty in April 2005 and are on course for EU membership in 2007, which has been their major strategic goal. The membership of both NATO and the EU will help to integrate these countries more fully into the wider Euro-Atlantic community.

Romania and Bulgaria will make the Black Sea region a higher strategic priority for the EU and can function as a model of democratic transition, stability, and security enforcement for those areas further to the East. Enlargement to the Black Sea and the changing political geography also will pave the way for further extension of the East-West corridor and add a new component to the North-South corridor (Russia, Caspian Sea, and the Persian Gulf). The EU, which has been and still is less influential in the Black Sea area than Russia and the United States, will strengthen its strategic position in the Black Sea region and gain access to important navigable rivers that run into the Black Sea (the Danube, Dniestr, and Dnieper) through the membership of Romania and Bulgaria. This development could be significant also for the EU's relations with Russia, Ukraine, the southern Caucasus, and the western Balkans.

Turkey.

Turkey's geopolitical location long has been and still is of strategic significance for both the EU and the United States. Throughout the Cold War era, Turkey has been an important security actor in Europe, as a staunch ally of the United States and Western Europe. The emerging security threats of the current era and the shifting regional focus on both sides of the Atlantic still call for close incorporation of Turkey into transatlantic security frameworks.

On October 3, 2005, the EU decided to open accession talks with Turkey, yet the road ahead seems bumpy and uncertain for an eventual Turkish accession. This section deals with the implications for transatlantic security relations of Turkey's efforts to gain EU membership. It scrutinizes the impact of success or failure of an eventual EU accession of Turkey on the emergent European security structures and on the future transatlantic security relationship.

My thesis here is that, with Turkish accession negotiations now started, Turkey is likely to have a stronger voice in the future of the

European Security and Defence Policy (ESDP). Turkish membership in the EU would provide a stronger connection between NATO and the EU/ESDP and help reinforce strategic relations between these transatlantic actors. The policy outcome of such a scenario is beneficial for all transatlantic parties involved: it is in the interest of Turkey from the perspective of increased political influence in both the development of ESDP and shaping of the dynamics of the region it is located in; it is in the interest of the EU from the perspective of having increased soft power in the Middle East and more effective and efficient response mechanisms in humanitarian crises on the European continent and elsewhere; and finally, it is in the national interest of the United States from the perspective of a more reliable strategic partnership and increased burden-sharing across the Atlantic.

TURKEY, RUSSIA, AND STICKY INSTITUTIONS: WHY THE TRANSATLANTIC SECURITY RELATIONSHIP ENDURES — AND SOME THOUGHTS ON FUTURE MISSIONS

Patrick B. Baetjer

The Future of Transatlantic Security Relations Conference that took place at Texas A&M University on March 8, 2006, afforded scholars and practitioners the opportunity to assess the status and strength of the relationship between Europe and the United States. Participants came from a variety of different organizations, countries, and theoretical persuasions, yet despite this diversity of viewpoints, five distinct and identifiable questions concerning the transatlantic relationship emerged. The interplay of discussions of history, current events, and future concerns about foreign, defense, and social policies among the United States, the European Union (EU), the North Atlantic Treaty Organization (NATO), and Russia materialized as major areas of interest throughout the conference. How the EU would handle Turkey's request to be a member of the EU, and the implications for NATO were major questions. Why NATO and the transatlantic relationship had endured beyond the end of the Cold War, and whether it would continue to do so were yet other areas of inquiry. Finally, NATO's future roles and missions received significant attention as well.

Whither the Relationship between NATO, the EU, the United States, and Russia?

A major set of underlying questions included the future relationships among nations and institutions, especially NATO, the EU, the United States, Western and Eastern European states, as well as Russia and the Ukraine. Several participants warned that, with the current emphasis on terrorism and the Middle East, the danger exists that Russia and the transatlantic relationship might be ignored. One of the fundamental difficulties broached is how NATO and Russia deal with one another. After all, NATO was formed on

April 4, 1949, as a measure of collective security against any potential Soviet aggression. The Soviet Union established its own alliance, the Warsaw Pact, in 1955 to counter NATO. Yet former Soviet satellites such as Hungary have joined NATO following the end of the Cold War. It remains unclear, however, whether the alliance's continued expansion eventually will cause alarm in Moscow, and what the Russians response will be. Whether the Russians continue to see NATO as a threat is an open question.

Some scholars suggest offering Russia NATO membership as a means to tie former Cold War enemies together. Dr. Josef Joffe opposed the suggestion, asserting that Russia's inclusion would unravel NATO. Joffe explained that, while Russia may not appear to harbor any renewed expansionist goals, the former Soviet satellite countries that have been free for less than 20 years remain suspicious about Russia's future intentions. Membership in NATO represents a guarantee that Russia will not be able to dominate or exert overweening influence yet again. Furthermore, NATO membership is seen as a break with the Soviet past and identification with the west. Admitting Russia, in this view, would do much to undermine the importance of NATO to its newest Eastern European members.

As in the case of NATO expansion, the Russian response to the enlargement of the EU continues to be unclear. While the EU lacks the military component found in NATO, it still represents an organization spreading eastwards that Russia has little ability to influence. There clearly is no support for even mentioning Russia as a candidate for inclusion in the EU for several reasons. Europe appears to have pushed for expansion too fast and too hard, leaving its population feeling "exhausted with expansion." Russia, once seen as on its way to becoming a democratic, law-abiding, capitalist state, may be backsliding toward authoritarianism and renewed state centralization. President Vladimir Putin has centralized a great deal of power in his hands, while eviscerating political opponents and the independent news media. The state, under the direction of Putin, has reseized various companies and industries from individuals like Mikhail Khodorkovsky, claiming that the sales of such assets in the 1990s amounted to robbery, and that many companies owed taxes. Other commentators suggest that the seizures were aimed at quieting

Russia's wealthy oligarchs, who had begun to use their resources to oppose Putin politically. Russia also is engaged in a "dirty war" in Chechnya, utilizing a variety of tactics that grossly violate human rights. Russia as an EU candidate, therefore, may be well beyond the realm of current possibilities.

While there is a track record of previous cooperation between the EU and Russia, most notably in the efforts to convince Iran to suspend its uranium enrichment program, such cooperation does not mean that Russia wields any significant direct influence within the EU. Energy is the one area where Russia could seek to exert greater influence over the behavior of the EU. Its state-owned energy company, Gazprom, exports a great deal of natural gas to Europe, while European demand keeps rising. Some officials suggest that Gazprom could capture one-third of the European natural gas market in the next 10 years.[1] Whether or not Russia could or would use energy to influence the expansion or behavior of the EU remains to be seen.

Relations between Russia and the United States have declined following a promising start. President George W. Bush famously stated that he looked into Putin's eyes, saw his soul, and was convinced that he was a man who would encourage greater cooperation between the United States and Russia. For his part, Putin was among the first to call Bush following the September 11, 2001 (9/11), terror attacks and offered whatever support he could provide. Russia was considered a staunch supporter of the War on Terror. Yet the United States has become frustrated by what it sees as Russia's attempts to stifle the democratic Rose and Orange Revolutions in Georgia and Ukraine, respectively. Furthermore, having declared itself a supporter of the War on Terror, Russia recast the war in Chechnya as a counterterrorist effort, while continuing to violate human rights on a large scale. Putin's efforts to wipe out the political opposition, his centralization of power, and his seizure of certain private companies all brought criticism from a disillusioned Bush White House. Recently, although the United States has supported the EU3 negotiations and Russia's attempts to convince the Iranians to suspend their nuclear enrichment programs, these Western efforts have been frustrated by the Russians, who reportedly signaled that they would veto any sanctions or military action against Iran in the United Nations (UN) Security Council.

It is unclear what Russia's future role will be or how it will react to the growth of the EU and NATO. Under Putin, Russia has shown signs of wanting to exert greater influence on world affairs than under Boris Yeltsin. Some suggest that Russia's attempts to influence events in former Soviet countries like Georgia and Ukraine indicate that Russia views NATO and the EU at least as competitors, if not threats. Continued diplomatic efforts are necessary to gauge Russian perceptions of threats and opportunities, and to make evident to Russia what the transatlantic alliance sees as its vital and important interests and values.

Whither the Relationship between NATO, the EU, the United States, and Turkey?

Much depends on how Europe handles its negotiations with Turkey on admittance to the EU. From Europe's perspective, its citizens appear to have been exhausted by the strains of rapid expansion. In some European countries, there is an undercurrent of skepticism concerning the entire EU concept. The rejection of the EU draft constitution in some countries was taken as a sign of this exhaustion. Long-time members of the EU have expressed concern that the newer Eastern European members, especially Poland, would flood the Western European members with poor, uneducated, and unemployed immigrants. They express fear that this would burden the much-beloved social welfare systems of many of these countries, while driving up the unemployment rate within each country. While this has not occurred so far, the concern is very much alive. In the case of Turkey, it is a much larger and a far poorer country than the EU previously has admitted.

The debate over the use of Islamic headscarves in French schools, the violent riots outside of Paris, the murder of Theo Van Gogh, the rail bombings in Madrid, and the bombings in London raise questions for many Europeans as to whether Muslim immigrants are willing to assimilate or even capable of doing so. Skeptics point to the large Muslim ghettos in Holland and France. Furthermore, with the rise of parties like the National Front in France and the British National Party, anti-immigrant feelings appear to be intensifying in Europe.

Concerned European political elites wonder whether Turkey, if admitted, would clamor for a voting system that favors population size over other factors. These elites fear that Turkey would call for an EU Assembly with a weighted voting system that gave more votes to the more populous member countries at the expense of the aging nations, thereby reducing the influence and status of long-time EU stalwarts such as France, Germany, and Italy.

Yet European concerns center on more than just what could happen if Turkey gained entry. Turkey was confronted with a whole raft of reforms that it needed to implement in order to begin accession negotiations. There is little evidence that Turkey has made much headway with most of the proposed reforms, and there are some indications that the country has moved in the opposite direction. Prognosticators suggest that should Prime Minister Recep Tayyip Erdogan's Justice and Development Party (AK) win the next election, he very well might move to weaken laws that have helped make Turkey a secular state.[2] Europeans see all of these trends, combined with the rise of Islamic fundamentalism, as worrisome and threatening to their national security and politics, and even to their fundamental social fabric. In short, critics contend that Turkey has not demonstrated an improved respect for human rights, that abuses by the security forces abound, and that the state may try to pass an anti-terror bill that would curtail free speech severely and expand police powers. Considering also several troubling interactions with Hamas, Syria, and Iran, many Europeans do not believe that Turkey has held up its end of the bargain.

Turkey argues that it has made progress, and that it has a lot to offer the EU. Panelist Oya Dursun suggested that it would be a public relations coup for the EU to admit a large Muslim nation to the club. She explained that much of the Muslim world sees the EU as a primarily white Christian organization, fueling the belief that the West and the Islamic world are headed for a clash of civilizations. Admittance would dissipate this belief. Turkey could act as a credible arbiter on behalf of Europe in efforts to bring the Israeli/Palestinian conflict to a close and could provide much-needed cultural sensitivity to issues involving the Muslim world and Europe.

Ms. Dursun suggested that Turkey would be content even if the EU did not grant the nation full member status. She envisioned some kind of "privileged partner" status for Turkey should full membership not be awarded. Ms. Dursun did not touch on the economic benefits of bringing Turkey into the EU. Much of Western Europe is aging, and it is incapable of replenishing its work force with young people. In time, Western Europe will be faced with declining productivity coupled with soaring social welfare costs of the aging populace. Turkey has a number of young unemployed potential workers who are mostly enthusiastic about integration into Europe, and who are typically educated and embrace the essence of the Western social contract necessary for living and working in a secular state. Like it or not, Europe cannot follow anti-immigration policies while holding on to expansive—and expensive—welfare programs. Turkey's young and underemployed population could hold the key.

Relations between Turkey and the United States have been up and down, with the low point coming in 2003 when Turkey refused to grant overflight rights or to permit a U.S. armored division to travel across Turkish territory to attack northern Iraq. Turkey remains very concerned about the situation in Iraq, fearing that the autonomous Kurdish region near Kirkuk eventually may push for independence. With between 6 and 12 million Kurds in Turkey, the state is concerned that the Kurds might try to carve out a larger state that would include northern Iraq and part of southern Turkey. The existence of a violent Kurdish separatist movement, the PKK, only exacerbates these concerns. Turkey is wary of the close relationship that has developed between the United States and the Kurds, beginning with Operation PROVIDE COMFORT in the 1990s and continuing with the joint operations launched by the U.S. military and the Kurdish peshmerga in Iraq today. Moreover, instability in Iraq brings smugglers, arms dealers, drug runners, and would-be insurgents across Turkey's border.

The United States, like the EU, has expressed concern over Turkish Prime Minister Erdogan's efforts to weaken the laws that have been in place since Ataturk to ensure a secular state. Like the Europeans, the United States deplores the continued human rights abuses and the repression of the Kurds. Yet the United States faces a conundrum with regard to Turkey's government. Though it is an avowed secular democracy, the Turkish military has intervened at times when Islamist candidates won elections, most recently in 1980 and 1997. While highly undemocratic, military interference in national politics has ensured the survival of a secular Turkish state. Complicating matters further, the same military that is the ultimate guarantor of secularism also has been implicated in some of the worst human rights abuses in Turkey. Thus questions about the Kurds, democracy, human rights, and the denial of overflight rights have led to a rocky relationship between the United States and Turkey.

Should the EU deny Turkey admission, it would likely impinge on NATO in some fashion. Turkey became a member of NATO on February 18, 1952, and maintains the largest number of troops among member states after the United States. Turkey proved a staunch ally throughout the Cold War, even allowing the United States to station *Jupiter* nuclear missiles on its territory. Yet rejection from the EU likely would strain Turkey's relations with NATO's European members. Turkey might prove less willing to contribute to NATO operations, particularly if it is European states which are pushing for a particular deployment. It is unlikely that a rejection from the EU would encourage Turkey to sever its ties with NATO, but it would be likely to make the country less enthusiastic about NATO deployments and cause further strains within the transatlantic alliance. Big questions therefore remain as to the potential for future improvements in Transatlantic-Middle Eastern regional relationships, as well as the possibilities for a significant Turkish role in improving ties among the Islamic and Western nations and cultures.

Whither NATO and the Transatlantic Relationship?

The conference panelists reached a general consensus about why the alliance has lasted and the prospects for its future. In general, the participants concluded that relatively close collaboration would continue into the future, this being the result of existing political and security institutions. Dr. Christopher Layne was the one noted exception; he viewed institutions as means by which the United States sought to impose its hegemony on the rest of the world. Yet nearly every panelist at some point acknowledged that such institutions had bound Europe and the United States together, and that NATO was an example of such an institution. This is not to say that participants agreed on exactly what the vital institutions were, or on whether the partnership needed improving.

Dr. Michael Brenner emphasized that Europe and the United States shared social institutions that accounted for the ongoing cooperation. Dr. Guillaume Parmentier argued that institutions explained past collaborative efforts, but that in the future, NATO should redefine itself as a coalition-enabling organization, and that another institution should be created to facilitate understanding between Europe and the United States. Dean Steinberg argued that U.S. policy had done much to strain institutions, but that U.S. foreign policy appeared to be improving in that regard. Dr. Josef Joffe likened the current incarnation of NATO to that of a market or bazaar, a place with many floors and a menu of capabilities to meet the myriad new challenges that NATO was not expected to meet during the Cold War. Dr. Joffe cautioned observers not to expect NATO to engage in large-scale conventional warfare, as it was originally founded for, but rather to focus more on humanitarian missions and perhaps stability operations.

Dr. Michael Desch pressed Dr. Joffe on the utility of such an organization, likening NATO to the New York City social registry, an antiquated club that has little relevant impact. Dr. Joffe replied that, while the capabilities of the registry were not what they once were, there was still a large number of people who wanted to be a part of it. NATO's most important feature may be that it is seen as a forum for the United States and Europe to discuss strategic issues, as well as for other nations, e.g., the Eastern Europeans, who still clamor to be a part of such exchanges.

The panelists touched on an ongoing debate in the academic world about the utility of institutions in international politics. To those who believe that institutions bring stability and lessen the chance for conflict between nations, institutions enable the predominant nations to "lock in" rules that all nations will agree to play by. Weaker nations agree to these rules because such rules restrain the power of the stronger nations and greatly decrease the chance that weaker nations will be abandoned or dominated.[3] Furthermore, institutions give weaker states a say and a stake in the international order above what their own relative power normally would enable them to have. Former U.S. Secretary of State Henry Kissinger once observed, "When we built the Atlantic alliance in the 1940s, Europe was very weak. And yet we gave it a status and a degree of participation [in the alliance] that went beyond what it could have demanded for itself. This should be one of our objectives with Russia."[4]

Dominant nations voluntarily agree to restraints on their power because, otherwise, the costs of staying dominant are extremely high, and weaker nations have an incentive to move to counterbalance them, thus decreasing the period of dominance of the stronger. NATO represents one such institution. Dr. Joffe commented, "The genius of American diplomacy was building institutions, from the UN to the IMF [International Monetary Fund], from NATO [to] the WTO. . . . They advanced American interests by serving those of others."[5]

Indeed, Dr. Joffe appears to argue that institutions are a far better means than soft power to ameliorate the points of conflict between Europe and the United States. Soft power, the attractiveness of a nation's culture and ideals, provides no sure access to increased influence over an admiring country. Joffe asserts, "Soft power does not necessarily increase the world's love for America. It is still power, and it can make enemies."[6] Soft power can convey a sense of cultural dominance, and he suggests that this could lead to a reactive, resentful government policy by a dominated party. One example is the "cultural exception" that France wrung from the EU free trade rule-makers in 1993. An EU state may go against free trade policy if that state seeks to protect or promote an endangered aspect of its culture. This was seen widely as a slight directed at the United States, with some Europeans suggesting that American culture was "hyped or heisted".[7]

Institutions have an additional advantage in that once created, member states find it very difficult to disentangle themselves from them. They provide states with a platform on which to conduct business with other states. John Ikenberry dubbed this concept institutional "stickiness."[8] States become so bound by institutions that they find it difficult to leave. Moreover, they find it difficult to gain an advantage over other member states. Ikenberry writes, "When political institutions are deeply entrenched and difficult to overturn or replace, this also reduces the returns on power and increases the continuity of the existing order."[9] Stickiness and the reduced return on power provide a plausible explanation for why NATO and the transatlantic relationship have endured beyond the end of the Cold War.

What Is NATO's Future Role and What Will Its Mission Be?

Conference participants came to a variety of conclusions about NATO's future roles and missions. Dr. Parmentier envisioned NATO as a coalition-enabling organization in which member states that had the will and capacity to act to confront an agreed-upon challenge could self-organize and mutually coordinate. He did not, however, indicate what measures could be taken to prevent the emergence of future "coalitions of the willing" that might enrage member states, as with what happened regarding Iraq.

Colonel William Gallagher's focus on the training of Eastern European militaries suggests that NATO could have a role in providing the necessary training for former Eastern Bloc countries who want to professionalize and modernize their armed forces. Such training would also establish contacts within the various militaries, opening lines of communication that could prove valuable if a crisis develops. General Ivany stated that the democratization of former Soviet satellite armies is certainly an important and ongoing mission.

Dr. Joffe seemed to suggest that NATO is the perfect institution through which to lock in the democratic advances in former Eastern Bloc countries, and that the alliance provides them with a measure of assurance that Russia can no longer wield the coercive influence over them that it once did. Furthermore, NATO features a number of capabilities that make it the perfect complement to the overwhelming technological power of the United States. As a "bazaar," NATO has experience with stability operations, providing security for elections, means for disarming rivals, and humanitarian assistance. NATO may not be able to fight the conventional war it was originally designed for, but its capabilities are still useful.

Finally, Dr. David McIntyre and Colonel Randy Larsen's Atlantic Storm and Dark Winter simulations revealed just how unprepared the transatlantic alliance is for a biological attack or outbreak. Coordination and pooling of necessary resources were revealed to be nearly nonexistent. The underlying message was that this could be an area that NATO focuses on, but, in that case, there is a great deal of planning that needs to begin immediately.

Conclusion.

The conference participants' presentations generally focused on four main questions: What will relations between the EU, the United States, NATO, and Russia look like; what will relations between Turkey, the EU, the United States, and NATO look like; why has NATO and the transatlantic partnership endured and will it continue to do so; and what are NATO's future roles and missions? Relations with Russia will depend largely on whether Russia views the enlargement of the EU and NATO as a threat. Relations with Turkey depend heavily on whether it is admitted to the EU. NATO has endured largely because international institutions have value and because of the concept of stickiness. Finally, NATO will play a variety of roles, but it will never again resemble the conventional warfighting organization it was designed to be at the onset of the Cold War.

ENDNOTES

1. "Who's Afraid of Gazprom?" *The Economist*, May 6-12, 2006, p. 61.

2. "Flying in the Wrong Direction," *The Economist*, May 6-12, 2006, p. 51.

3. G. John Ikenberry, *After Victory: Institutions, Strategic Restraint, and the Rebuilding of Order After Major Wars*, Princeton: Princeton University Press, 2001, p. 258.

4. Quoted in Fareed Zakaria, "America's New Balancing Act," *Newsweek*, August 6, 2001.

5. *Ibid.*

6. Josef Joffe, "The Perils of Soft Power," *New York Times Magazine*, May 14, 2006.

7. *Ibid.*

8. Ikenberry, p. 5.

9. *Ibid.*, p. 266.

PARTICIPANT BIOGRAPHIES

PATRICK B. BAETJER is originally from Unionville, Pennsylvania. He worked in the United States Senate before moving to the Center for Strategic and International Studies as a Research Assistant to the Arleigh A. Burke Chair in Strategy. Mr. Baetjer's work focused on the Middle East, especially Iran and Iraq, terrorism, and military force transformation. He assisted in the research and writing of *Iraqi Security Forces: A Strategy for Success* by Dr. Anthony Cordesman. Mr. Baetjer is a student in the George Bush School of Government and Public service pursuing a degree in International Affairs. He received a B.A. in History from Davidson College.

MICHAEL BRENNER teaches American foreign policy, international relations theory, international political economy, and national security at the Graduate School of Public and International Affairs at the University of Pittsburgh. He has been a consultant with the U.S. Department of Defense and the Foreign Service Institute and has published a number of works, including *Europe's New Security Vocation*, *Reconcilable Differences: US-French Relations in the New Era* with Guillaume Parmentier, *Terms of Engagement*, *The US and European Security Identity*, and "Kritischer Dialog oder Konstruktives Engagement?" *Internationale Politik* (Bonn, September 1997). Dr. Brenner received his doctorate in political science from the University of California at Berkeley.

JOSEPH R. CERAMI was appointed as a Lecturer in National Security Policy for the Bush School of Government and Public Service, Texas A&M University, in 2001. During a 30-year military career, Colonel Cerami served in Germany, the Republic of Korea, and the United States as a Field Artillery officer, operational planner, and strategist. His last assignment was as the Chairman of the Department of National Security and Strategy at the U.S. Army War College, Carlisle Barracks, Pennsylvania, from 1998 to 2001. From 1993 to 1998, he served on the faculty there as Director of International Security Studies. From 1980 to 1983, he was Assistant Professor of Political Science at the U.S. Military Academy, West Point, New York, where he taught International Relations, and Politics and Government. Colonel Cerami has published numerous articles on defense policy and, along with Colonel James F. Holcomb, Jr., he is co-editor of the *Army War College Guide to Strategy*. He has a B.S. in Engineering from the U.S. Military Academy at West Point, an M.A. in Government from the University of Texas at Austin, and an MMAS in Theater Operations from the School of Advanced Military Studies at Fort Leavenworth, Kansas. He is also a graduate of the Army War College. In 1995 Colonel Cerami was awarded a Certificate from the John F. Kennedy School of Government, Harvard University, Program for Senior Officials in National Security.

RICHARD A. CHILCOAT retired from the U.S. Army after 42 years of active military service on September 1, 2000. During his military career, he served in a variety of leadership positions, including Chief of Staff, 3d Infantry Division, in Germany; Executive Assistant to General Colin Powell, Chairman of the Joint Chiefs of Staff; Deputy Director, Strategy, Plans, and Policy, Office of the Deputy Chief of Staff for Operations and Plans; and Senior Speechwriter to the Army Chief of Staff, General John A. Wickham, Jr. He served as Assistant to the Academy Dean, Assistant Professor of Social Sciences, and member of the Academy Athletic Board at the U.S. Military Academy. In 1994, Lieutenant General Chilcoat became the 43d Commandant of the U.S. Army War College. In 1997, he was appointed ninth President of the National Defense University by the Chairman of the Joint Chiefs of Staff, serving until July 7, 2000. On July 1, 2001, he was named Dean of the George Bush School of Government and Public Service, at Texas A&M University. Currently, he serves as a member of the Board of Advisors, CIA University, Class Trustee of the Association of Graduates, U.S. Military Academy, and member of the Board of Directors, National Defense University Foundation. Lieutenant General Chilcoat received his M.B.A. from Harvard Business School and B.S. from the U.S. Military Academy. He is an honorary graduate of the U.S. Army War College.

READ DEAL joined the Bush School from the defense industry where he worked as a Senior Business Analyst at Northrop Grumman Corporation. He began work for Northrop Grumman upon receiving his M.B.A. from the Cox School of Business at SMU and his bachelor's degree from Dickinson College. Mr. Deal is a master's degree candidate in the Bush School International Affairs program studying national security issues.

MICHAEL DESCH was named the first holder of the Robert M. Gates Chair in Intelligence and National Security Decision-Making at the George Bush School of Government and Public Service at Texas A&M University in 2004. Prior to that, he was Professor and Director of the Patterson School of Diplomacy and International Commerce at the University of Kentucky. From 1993 through 1998, he was Assistant Director and Senior Research Associate at the Olin Institute. He teaches courses in national security policy, political theory and international relations, and democracy and American foreign policy.

ALAN DOBSON taught at the University of Wales Swansea from 1978 to 1999 in the Department of Political Theory and Government. In 1999 he was appointed to the Chair of Politics at Dundee and in 2003 became Director of the Faculty's Institute for Transatlantic European and American Studies. Dr. Dobson is a Fellow of the Royal Historical Society and for several years a Fellow of the Royal Aeronautical Society. In 1997 he was a Senior Research Fellow at the Norwegian Nobel Institute in Oslo, and in October 2005 held the Lenna Fellowship at the University of St. Bonaventure, New York. Dr. Dobson has published three books on Anglo-American relations and two on the international airline system, co-authored a book on U.S. foreign policy, and edited a collection of essays on the Cold War. He has published numerous articles in leading international relations and history journals. Dr. Dobson received his doctorate at the University of Durham and an MSc in International Politics at the University of Southampton.

OYA DURSUN is an Assistant Instructor in the Department of Government at the University of Texas at Austin. Her teaching experience includes positions as Adjunct Professor in the Department of Political Science and International Relations in Boğaziçi University in Turkey, Summer 2005; and as a Visiting Professor in the Department of International Relations at Lodz Academy of International Studies in Lodz, Poland, Spring 2005. Ms. Dursun has been published by the Bologna Center Journal of International Affairs, the United Nations Press, and the Referans Gazetesi, and has several other publications accepted for publication by the *French Politics*, the *LBJ Journal of Public Affairs*, and the EU Center of Excellence at Texas A&M University. Ms. Dursun also received the Patterson Fellowship at the University of Texas at Austin, 2005; was in the Erasmus-Socrates Scholar Program, 2005; and had a Deutscher Academischer Austausch Dienst (DAAD) fellowship for studying in Germany, 2004. She is a Ph.D. candidate on comparative politics, international relations, and American politics at the University of Texas at Austin.

JEFFREY A. ENGEL is Assistant Professor, Bush School, where he teaches courses in American foreign policy and the evolution of international strategy. Before coming to the Bush School, he was a lecturer in History and International Relations at the University of Pennsylvania (2003-04), a Visiting Assistant Professor at Haverford College (2004), and an Olin Postdoctoral Fellow in International Security Studies at Yale University (2001-03). Dr. Engel edited a collection detailing the local impact of Cold War diplomacy and currently is completing a book on aircraft sales, export controls, and trading with adversaries during the Cold War. Dr. Engel received his Ph.D. in American history from the University of Wisconsin-Madison.

WILLIAM J. GALLAGHER is the Chief of Staff for Strategic Operations, Multi-National Force-Iraq and is assigned in Baghdad. Previously, he was the Chief of the Initiatives Group for the U.S. Army, Europe, located in Heidelberg, Germany. Colonel Gallagher has served over 25 years in a variety of command and staff assignments as an Army infantry officer. He was a National Security Fellow at Harvard University and is a graduate of West Point. Colonel Gallagher holds a Bachelor of Science degree in engineering, an MBA, and an MA in leadership development.

KLAUS-PETER GOTTWALD has been Deputy Chief of Mission of the German Embassy in Washington since July 7, 2003. Just before his appointment to Washington, Mr. Gottwald was a fellow at the Weatherhead Center for International Affairs of Harvard University. His most recent position at the Foreign Office in Berlin was as director for North America from 1998 to 2002. At the Foreign Office, he also served as a deputy spokesman for former Foreign Minister Hans-Dietrich Genscher and as deputy director in the arms control and disarmament division. Overseas, Mr. Gottwald served in London from 1993 to 1998, first on secondment to the British Foreign and Commonwealth Office, policy planning staff, and then as head of the press and public information department of the German Embassy. Additional foreign assignments include the political department of the German Embassy in Washington, where he worked on political/military affairs and arms control issues from 1987 to 1990; head of the press department of the German Embassy in Helsinki; and work with the German UNESCO delegation in Paris. Mr. Gottwald joined the German Foreign Service in 1977. Prior to his career there, he worked as head of the United Nations Development Program (UNDP) in the UNDP's regional office in Kaduna, northern Nigeria. Mr. Gottwald was educated at the universities of Mannheim, Frankfurt, and Konstanz (degree in social sciences/public administration) and holds an M.A. in international relations from Syracuse University.

DANIEL HAMILTON is the Richard von Weizsäcker Professor and Director of the Center for Transatlantic Relations at the Paul H. Nitze School of Advanced International Studies (SAIS), Johns Hopkins University; and Executive Director of the American Consortium on EU Studies (ACES), a cooperative venture among five major universities in the nation's capital designated by the European Commission as the EU Center of Excellence, Washington, DC. Dr. Hamilton is publisher of *Transatlantic: Europe, America & the World*, the Center's bimonthly magazine on transatlantic issues. He leads the international policy work of the Johns Hopkins-based U.S. National Center of Excellence on Homeland Security, awarded by the U.S. Department of Homeland Security. Dr. Hamilton has held a variety of senior positions in the U.S. Department of State, including Deputy Assistant Secretary for European Affairs, responsible for NATO, OSCE, and transatlantic security issues, Balkan stabilization, and Northern European issues; U.S. Special Coordinator for Southeast

European Stabilization; Associate Director of the Policy Planning Staff; and Senior Policy Advisor to the U.S. Ambassador and U.S. Embassy in Germany. From 1990 to 1993, he was Senior Associate on European-American relations at the Carnegie Endowment for International Peace. From 1982 to 1990, he was Deputy Director of the Aspen Institute Berlin. Dr. Hamilton has a Ph.D. and M.A. with distinction from the Johns Hopkins School of Advanced International Studies, with a concentration in U.S. Foreign Policy, European Studies, and International Economics. He was awarded a Doctorate of Humanities h.c. by Concordia College in May 2002. He received his B.S.F.S magna cum laude at Georgetown University's School of Foreign Service, and studied at the University of Konstanz and at St. Olaf College.

CHARLES HERMANN is a professor of Political Science at Texas A&M University. In addition to serving as the Interim Associate Dean for Academic Programs and Associate Dean for International Affairs of the Bush School, Dr. Hermann teaches the gateway course for the International Affairs Track—Problems in Contemporary U.S. Foreign Policy. In 1969, he left Princeton University to serve on the National Security Council staff under Dr. Henry Kissinger. Before coming to Texas A&M in 1995, Dr. Hermann served as Director of the Mershon Center, a think tank on international security and public policy located at Ohio State University, where he also spent several years as Associate Provost for International Affairs. Dr. Hermann is a past president of the International Studies Association and a principal investigator for research grants from such sources as the National Science Foundation, U.S. Arms Control and Disarmament Agency, the Department of Defense, the Hewlett Foundation, and the MacArthur Foundation. An active scholar in the fields of foreign policy, national security policy, and group decisionmaking, his recent publications include the editorship of *The American Defense Annual* and *New Directions in Foreign Policy*. Dr. Hermann received his Ph.D. in political science from Northwestern University.

ROBERT IVANY became the eighth president of the University of St. Thomas on July 1, 2004. Prior to his retirement from the Army with the rank of Major General, Dr. Ivany was Commandant of the U.S. Army

War College in Carlisle, Pennsylvania. There for 3 years, he instituted programs to develop the next generation of military and civilian leaders from the United States and 42 foreign countries to meet the challenges of cultural change, organizational transformation, and a drastically altered national security environment. During his various commands as an armored cavalry officer, he led soldiers in the United States, Kuwait, Saudi Arabia, the Federal Republic of Germany, and Vietnam, where he was wounded in action and decorated for valor. During his distinguished Army career, he assisted several nations in the transformation of their armed forces. In 1990, Dr. Ivany was the first senior military officer invited to Hungary to contribute to the democratization of their defense establishment. He lived in Saudi Arabia and Kuwait, advising military and civilian leaders on the modernization of their military forces following Operation DESERT STORM. In Kuwait, he headed the American effort with a team of 45 advisors managing a $1.2 billion program to improve their education, training, and logistics. Dr. Ivany also served in a number of unique positions including the Army Aide to the President of the United States from 1984 to 1986 and an assistant professor of history and assistant football coach at the Military Academy at West Point. As the Commanding General of the Military District of Washington, he directed a diverse organization of 5,500 civilian and military employees based on seven installations in three states and the District of Columbia. In addition to earning a B.S. degree from the U.S. Military Academy, Dr. Ivany received a Ph.D. in History from the University of Wisconsin in Madison.

JOSEF JOFFE is publisher-editor of the German weekly *Die Zeit*. Previously he was columnist/editorial page editor of *Süddeutsche Zeitung* (1985–2000). Dr. Joffe's essays and reviews have appeared widely in such publications as the *New York Review of Books*, *Times Literary Supplement*, *Commentary*, *New York Times Magazine*, *New Republic*, *Weekly Standard*, and the *Prospect* (London). He is a regular contributor to metropolitan daily newspapers in the United States and Britain. Dr. Joffe's second career has been in academia. Currently, he is adjunct professor of political science at Stanford, where he was the Payne Distinguished Lecturer (1999-2000). He also is a distinguished fellow of the Freeman Spogli Institute for International Studies at

Stanford. In 1990–91, Dr. Joffe taught at Harvard, where he is also an associate of the Olin Institute for Strategic Studies. He was a visiting lecturer in 2002 at Dartmouth College and in 1998 at Princeton University's Woodrow Wilson School. He was a professorial lecturer at Johns Hopkins School of Advanced International Studies in 1982–84. Dr. Joffe's scholarly work has appeared in many books and in journals such as *Foreign Affairs*, the *National Interest*, *International Security*, and *Foreign Policy*, as well as in professional journals in Germany, Britain, and France. He is the author of *The Limited Partnership: Europe, the United States and the Burdens of Alliance* and coauthor of *Eroding Empire: Western Relations with Eastern Europe*. His most recent book is *The Future of International Politics: The Great Powers* (1998); forthcoming is *Über-Power: The Imperial Temptation in American Foreign Policy*, to be published by W.W. Norton. Among his many awards are honorary doctoral degrees in humane letters from Swarthmore College in 2002 and Lewis and Clark College in 2005; the Theodor Wolff Prize (journalism), Ludwig Börne Prize (essays/literature), and the Federal Order of Merit, Germany. Dr. Joffe received his Ph.D. in government from Harvard University.

SAMUEL A. KIRKPATRICK is Executive Associate Dean for Academic Affairs and Management and Executive Professor at the Bush School of Government and Public Service at Texas A&M University. Immediately prior to rejoining Texas A&M, he was a Senior Fellow at the American Association of State Colleges and Universities in Washington, DC, where he advised university presidents, and engaged in public university projects relevant to the metropolitan mission, public engagement, civic education, and cultural and economic development outreach. Dr. Kirkpatrick is also a Senior Fellow at Strategic Initiatives, Inc., where he provides consultative services in strategic planning, continuous quality improvement, change management, and technology innovations for nonprofit organizations. In addition, he serves as an advisor/Senior Executive to boards in the areas of fundraising and strategic planning and as an independent management consultant. Dr. Kirkpatrick has served as the president of two public universities that offer programs in the arts, sciences, and professions to more than 25,000 degree students and large numbers of nondegree students served by over 2,500 faculty and staff. Dr. Kirkpatrick received a Ph.D. and M.A. in political science from the Pennsylvania State University and a bachelor's degree and honorary doctorate in public service from Shippensburg University.

RANDALL J. LARSEN is the Director of the Institute for Homeland Security and a Senior Associate at the Center for Biosecurity, University of Pittsburgh Medical Center. A retired U.S. Air Force colonel, he previously served as the Chairman, Department of Military Strategy and Operations, at the National War College in Washington, DC. Since 2001 he has frequently served as an expert witness for the U.S. Congress on issues ranging from biological and nuclear terrorism to spending priorities and national strategies for homeland security. In March 2005, Colonel Larsen designed and led a 2-day workshop on the threat of nuclear and biological terrorism for the House Homeland Security Committee. For more than 3 years, he has served as the homeland security consultant to CBS News, and is also the co-host of public radio's weekly show, *Homeland Security: Inside and Out*. Colonel Gallagher's book, *Our Own Worst Enemy*, will be published by Warner books in 2007.

CHRISTOPHER LAYNE joined the Bush School Faculty in the Fall 2005. His fields of interest are international relations theory, U.S. foreign policy, and strategic studies. Previously, he has taught at the School of International Studies, University of Miami; the Naval Postgraduate School; and in the Department of Political Science, University of California, Los Angeles. Dr. Layne has held numerous research positions and has been the recipient of a Research and Writing Grant in Global Security from the John D. and Catherine T. MacArthur Foundation, and also has received research grants from the Smith Richardson Foundation and from the Earhart Foundation. Dr. Layne is the author of *The Peace of Illusions: American Grand Strategy from 1940 to the Present* (Cornell University Press, 2006). He practiced law for 10 years in Los Angeles, California, and served as law clerk to the late Richard A. Gadbois, Jr., U.S. District Judge for the Central District of California. Dr. Layne received his Ph.D. in political science from the University of California, Berkeley, a diploma in historical studies from Cambridge University, an LL.M. in international law from the University of Virginia Law School, a J.D. from the University of Southern California Law School, and a B.A. (Cum Laude) in International Relations from the University of Southern California.

JOHAN LEMBKE is Senior Lecturer at the George Bush School of Government and Public Service, teaching courses on transatlantic relations and the European Union to students in its master's degree in international affairs program, and Director of the European Union Center at the Texas A&M University in College Station. Dr. Lembke most recently served as Associate Professorial Lecturer at the Elliott School of International Affairs at George Washington University in Washington, DC, where he taught undergraduate and graduate courses in European foreign policy, European economic and security policy, high technology policy, international corporate strategies, international political economy, transatlantic relations, and specialized courses on the Baltic Sea region. Dr. Lembke received his doctorate in international political economy and political science from Stockholm University in Sweden, where he also taught International Relations. He also received a B.Sc. in security studies and political science and B.A. in romance languages from Stockholm University.

JAY LOCKENOUR is a Professor of History at Temple University in Philadelphia. He teaches courses on German history, modern European social and military history, and history and film. He has worked on a wide range of subjects, from German political culture and national identity, to POW and veterans' affairs, to the role of film in illuminating historical consciousness. Dr. Lockenour recently completed a book project that combines many of these interests by examining the material and ideological effects of World War II and its aftermath on former German officers living in the Federal Republic of Germany. He has two ongoing projects: a study of German war films that examines their role in shaping public memory of World War II, and a study of the military career and anti-Semitic politics of Erich Ludendorff. Dr. Lockenour has published several works, including *Soldiers as Citizens: German Veterans in the Federal Republic,*

1945-1955; "The Rift in Our Ranks: The German Officer Corps, the 20th of July, and the Path to Democracy," *German Studies Review* (October 1998), and "Black and White Memories of War: German 'War Movies' and Public Memory," paper delivered at the 1996 Annual Meeting of the Popular Culture Association/American Culture Association, March 27, 1996. Dr. Lockenour has received grants from the German Academic Exchange Service, the Mellon Foundation, and the Fulbright Commission.

DOUGLAS C. LOVELACE, JR., is Director of the Strategic Studies Institute at the U.S. Army War College. His Army career included a combat tour in Vietnam and a number of command and staff assignments. While serving in the Plans, Concepts, and Assessments Division and the Conventional War Plans Division of the Joint Staff, he collaborated in the development of documents such as the National Military Strategy, the Joint Strategic Capabilities Plan, the Joint Military Net Assessment, national security directives, and presidential decision directives. He also was Director of Military Requirements and Capabilities Management at the U.S. Army War College, held the Douglas MacArthur Professor of Research Chair, and served as Director of Research in the Strategic Studies Institute. Professor Lovelace has published extensively in the areas of national security and military strategy formulation, future military requirements, and strategic planning. Professor Lovelace is a graduate of the U.S. Army Command and General Staff College and the National War College. He holds an MBA from Embry Riddle Aeronautical University and a J.D. from Widener University School of Law and is a member of the Pennsylvania and New Jersey bars.

DAVID MCINTYRE directs the Bush School Certificate Program in Homeland Security and is the Director of the Integrative Center for Homeland Security for Texas A&M. Between 2001 and 2003, he served as Deputy Director of the ANSER Institute for Homeland Security, the nation's only not-for-profit think tank focused solely on homeland security. In 2001 Dr. McIntyre retired from the U.S. military as the Dean of Faculty at the National War College. His approach to strategic problem-solving is built on 6 years of practical experience writing for four-star military leaders, including the Army

Chief of Staff, and the Commander of all U.S. forces in the Asia-Pacific region. Dr. McIntyre holds a B.S. in engineering from West Point, an M.A. in English and American literature from Auburn University, and a Ph.D. in political science from the University of Maryland. He is a graduate of the U.S. Army War College and the National War College.

PLAMEN PANTEV is Founder and Director of the Institute for Security and International Studies (ISIS) in Sofia, Bulgaria, and an Associate Professor at Sofia University "St. Kliment Ohridsky." His international experience included IREX Researcher at Columbia University, New York; Johns Hopkins University, SAIS, Washington, DC; Harvard University, Law School in 1988-89; a NATO Individual Fellow in 1995-97; Ford Foundation/WEU Institute for Security Studies Fellow at the Istituto Affari Internazionali in Rome, Italy, 1992; Foreign Researcher at The Netherlands Institute for International Relations "Clingendael" in 1993; Consultant to the Delegation of the EC in Sofia on foreign and regional policy of Bulgaria (1997-2001); Sandhurst Academy, United Kingdom, in March 2001; NATO Defense College, Rome, Italy, in May 2002; the Henry L. Stimson Center, Washington, DC, in May 2003; the Diplomatic Academy, Vienna, Austria, in July 2004; and the Institute for European Policy, Berlin/Andrassy University, Budapest, Hungary, in September 2005. Dr. Pantev has authored more than 120 academic publications in the fields of international, regional, and national security, transatlantic relations, European Security and Defense Policy, international relations, international law, and international negotiations, in Bulgarian, English, Russian, French, and German.

GUILLAUME PARMENTIER is the Director of the French Center on the United States (CFE) at the French Institute of Internationale Relations (IFRI). He has conceived and initiated the Center on the United States and France at the Brookings Institution in Washington, DC, and of the French Center on the United States (CFE) at IFRI in Paris, of which he became the Director in 1999. From 1983, Mr. Parmentier was the Director of the Civilian Affairs Committee of the North Atlantic Assembly. He was Assistant Director of Information and Head of External Relations at the NATO headquarters (1990-94). Between 1995 and 1997, he was an advisor for international affairs at the French Defense Minister's *Cabinet*. He then became Director of Studies and Research at the French Foundation for Defense Studies (1997-99), which he left upon the creation of CFE. Dr. Parmentier was educated at the Universities of Cambridge and the Sorbonne and Sciences-Pô in Paris, and has published extensively on European and transatlantic issues.

JOHN PRIOR is currently assigned as a Strategist in the Strategy, Plans, and Policy Directorate, Headquarters, Department of the Army. He is the Program Manager for the Eisenhower National Security Series, a year-long series of forums designed to engage the national security community in a broad and unique dialogue that identifies and promotes new ways to focus national power to meet the full range of security challenges confronting the United States in the 21st century. Captain Prior's Army service includes duty as rifle platoon leader, antiarmor platoon leader, headquarters company executive officer, battalion logistics officer and assistant battalion operations officer for air operations in the 82nd Airborne Division, and assistant battalion operations officer and company commander in the 1st Armored Division, including 15 months of service during Operation IRAQI FREEDOM from March 2003 through June 2004. Captain Prior received a B.S. in mechanical engineering from Rose-Hulman Institute of Technology in Terre Haute, a Master of Science in engineering management from the University of Missouri at Rolla; and a Master of Public Administration from the John F. Kennedy School of Government, Harvard University.

BRADLEY SMITH, a molecular biologist and policy analyst, is an Associate at the Center for Biosecurity of UPMC, and an Assistant Professor at the University of Pittsburgh School of Medicine. His work at the Center focuses on improving the supply of medicines, vaccines, and other medical countermeasures for biosecurity threats. Dr. Smith is one of the principal organizers of the *Alliance for Biosecurity*, a collaboration between the Center and more than 10 biotechnology and pharmaceutical companies founded in 2005. He also is involved in strengthening international biosecurity preparedness, and served as the Project Director for the table-top bioterrorism exercise *Atlantic Storm*, whose scenario features a transatlantic summit of international leaders from Europe and North America responding to a campaign of bioterrorist attacks. Dr. Smith is an Associate Editor of the journal *Biosecurity and Bioterrorism: Biodefense Strategy, Practice, and Science*.

JAMES STEINBERG is the Dean and holder of the Pickle Regents Chair in Public Affairs of the Lyndon B. Johnson School of Public Affairs. Before joining the School, he was the vice president and director of Foreign Policy Studies at the Brookings Institution in Washington, DC (2001-05), where he supervised a wide-ranging research program on U.S. foreign policy. From December 1996 to August 2000, Dr. Steinberg served as deputy national security advisor to President Bill Clinton. During that period he also served as the president's personal representative ("sherpa") to the 1998 and 1999 G-8 summits. Prior to becoming deputy national security advisor, Dr. Steinberg served as chief of staff of the U.S. State Department and director of the State Department's policy planning staff (1994-96), and as deputy assistant secretary for analysis in the Bureau of Intelligence and Research (1993-94). He has also been a senior analyst at RAND in Santa Monica (1989-93), and a senior fellow for U.S. Strategic Policy at the International Institute for Strategic Studies in London (1985-87). Dr. Steinberg served as Senator Edward Kennedy's principal aide for the Senate Armed Services Committee (1983-85); minority counsel, U.S. Senate Labor and Human Resources Committee (1981-83); special assistant to the U.S. Assistant Attorney General (Civil Division) (1979-80); law clerk to Judge David L. Bazelon, U.S. Court of Appeals for the D.C. Circuit (1978-79); and special assistant to the assistant secretary for planning and evaluation, U.S. Department of Health, Education, and Welfare (1977). He also is a member of the board of directors of the Pacific Council on International Policy, the *Bulletin of Atomic Scientists*, the International Advisory Board for the International Programs Committee of the Governing Board of the National Research Council, and the President's Council on International Activities of Yale University. He is a member of the D.C. Bar. Dr. Steinberg received his bachelor's degree from Harvard in 1973 and a J.D. degree from Yale Law School in 1978.

RADBOUD J. H. M. VAN DEN AKKER currently is assigned to the Policy Planning and Speechwriting Section, Political Affairs and Security Policy Division, NATO Headquarters, where he writes speeches, articles, and think pieces for the NATO Secretary General and other senior NATO officials. He first joined NATO Headquarters at the end of 1992 as Executive Officer of the International Staff's Political Affairs Division, before moving to his current position in 1999. In Brussels, Mr. van den Akker first served on the International Secretariat of the NATO Parliamentary Assembly. As the Director of the Assembly's Economic Committee, he coordinated the work of a committee of over 50 parliamentarians from NATO country parliaments and, from 1989 onwards, Central and Eastern Europe, in areas of defense/economic aspects of the transatlantic relationship, and East-West economic cooperation and convergence. Mr. van den Akker received a B.A. in History and an M.A. in Modern History and International Relations from the Utrecht University, The Netherlands.

TYSON VOELKEL currently is a student in the George Bush School of Government and Public service pursuing a degree in International Affairs. After graduation, Captain Voelkel will serve as an instructor at the U.S. Military Academy at West Point. He served as a company commander in the 82nd Airborne Division on two separate tours to Iraq. Captain Voelkel graduated from Texas A&M University with a degree in engineering.

SPONSOR INFORMATION

The European Union Center of Excellence (EUCE) in the International Programs Office at Texas A&M University is a university-wide body devoted to studying European Union (EU) and transatlantic affairs. Established in 2001, it is a forum for active, balanced, and nonpartisan Euro-Atlantic dialogues through education, debate, scholarly inquiry, campus resources, community outreach, public service, and transatlantic collaboration. It is part of the EUCE Network in the United States and is the only such official center in the south-central and southwestern United States co-funded by the European Commission.

The EUCE pursues an integrated portfolio of initiatives in support of Texas A&M University's globalization efforts. It complements academic-educational programs and advocates scholarship across disciplinary and collegiate borders. It sponsors and stimulates a broad repertoire of events and initiatives such as conferences, lectures, panels, publications, business seminars, training for public schoolteachers, student and faculty research grants, scholars-in-residence, and curriculum enhancement. The EUCE focuses attention on themes such as climate change, energy, and the environment; knowledge and innovation; and shared safety and security. As its distinct profile, the EUCE pursues projects oriented towards the wider Baltic Sea, Black Sea, Mediterranean Sea, and Gulf of Mexico regions, and strategic implications of EU enlargement.

The EUCE brings together colleges, departments, and other entities on the campus and in the wider region, and works with faculty, students, and staff. It builds networks and collaborates with similar bodies in Europe through professional relationships to enhance the quality and impact of its initiatives. The EUCE reaches out to groups and individuals with varied backgrounds, experiences, and interests in the academic, corporate, educational, nonprofit, news media, and public affairs sectors and the broader community.

The George Bush Presidential Library Foundation was established in 1991 as a nonprofit educational foundation to design, build, and support the George Bush Presidential Library and Museum at Texas A&M University. In addition to sponsoring its own programs and activities, the Foundation provides program and financial support to the Library, as well as the George Bush School of Government and Public Service.

The Foundation sponsors a number of programs, including a yearly domestic and foreign policy conference, the White House Lecture and Exhibit Series, and various other lecture and program series. Through its newsletter and quarterly events flyer, the Foundation reaches out to the entire United States to attract participants to its activities. Through its activities, the Foundation is helping make the George Bush Presidential Library Center a leading center in cultural, policy, and academic dialogue.

The Bush School of Government and Public Service at Texas A&M University educates principled leaders in public and international affairs, conducts research, and performs service. Both the Master of Public Service and Administration (MPSA) and Master of International Affairs (MPIA) are full-time graduate degree programs that provide a professional education for individuals seeking careers in the public or nonprofit sectors, or for activities in the private sector that have a governmental focus. The curriculum integrates leadership assessment and skills training throughout the course of study. The leadership emphasis and required capstone project enhance students' skills in areas of critical importance to effective public management.

The MPSA, a 21-month, 48-credit-hour program, combines 11 courses in public management, policy analysis, economics, and research methods with six electives, two of which may be taken in other departments at Texas A&M University. These electives allow students to pursue interests and develop specialties throughout the wide range of activities encompassed by public service. Students select an elective concentration in one of the following areas: nonprofit organizations; state and local policy and management; natural resources, environment, and technology policy and administration; security, energy, and technology policy; and health policy and management. A professional internship is completed in the first summer session.

The MPIA, a 21-month, 48-credit-hour program, offers tracks in National Security Affairs and International Economics and Development. To refine study in either track, students construct a program of study based on two or more concentrations or clusters of related courses such as economic development, diplomacy in world affairs, intelligence in statecraft, national security, or regional studies. Classes are taught by a faculty with both scholarly and practical international experience. Satisfactory completion of a foreign language exam is required to graduate. At the end of their first year of study, students will participate in either an internationally-oriented internship or a foreign language immersion course.

Certificate programs are designed for individuals interested in advancing their understanding in the international or security arenas. The Certificate in Advanced International Affairs (CAIA) Program is a focused curriculum offered via distance education or through in-residence study. It is designed for people who have limited time but a strong need to upgrade specific dimensions of their understanding of international relations. Students take 12-15 credit hours of graduate course work in international affairs chosen from a menu of courses.

The Certificate in Homeland Security (CHS) Program is offered only via distance education and intended for people who need to understand the new security environment as part of their management and supervisory duties. This program requires students to take 15 credit hours of graduate course work centered upon homeland security issues and strategies at all levels of the government and private industry. Courses also cover terrorism, response and recovery to weapons of mass destruction, and critical infrastructure protection.

The Institute for Science, Technology & Public Policy (ISTPP) is a nonpartisan, interdisciplinary public policy research institute, which pursues the dual mission of examining public policy issues in scholarly depth, and communicating research-based knowledge to public and policy decisionmakers. ISTPP seeks to facilitate interdisciplinary research required for today's complex problems and enhance Texas A&M University's ability to communicate research findings in ways that have a positive impact on policy and public understanding of scientific and technological issues. Current research focus areas include Environmental and Natural Resources Policy; Infrastructure, Environment, and Public Policy; Biotechnology and Public Policy; and Information Technology and Public Policy.

The **Strategic Studies Institute** is the U.S. Army's center for geostrategic and national security research and analysis. The Strategic Studies Institute conducts strategic research and analysis to support the U.S. Army War College curricula, provides direct analysis for Army and Department of Defense leadership, and serves as a bridge to the wider strategic community.

The Strategic Studies Institute is composed of civilian research professors, uniformed military officers, and a professional support staff. All have extensive credentials and experience. SSI is divided into three components: the Art of War Department focuses on global, transregional, and functional issues, particularly those dealing with Army transformation; the Regional Strategy and Planning Department focuses on regional strategic issues; and the Academic Engagement Program creates and sustains partnerships with the global strategic community. In addition to its organic resources, SSI has a web of partnerships with strategic analysts around the world, including the foremost thinkers in the field of security and military strategy. In most years, about half of SSI's publications are written by these external partners.

SSI studies are published by the Institute and distributed to key strategic leaders in the Army and Department of Defense, the military educational system, Congress, the media, other think tanks and defense institutes, and major colleges and universities. SSI studies use history and current political, economic, and military factors to develop strategic recommendations.

- Books - SSI publishes about 3-5 books per year consisting of authored works or edited compilations.
- Monographs - Policy oriented reports that provide recommendations. They are usually 25-90 pages in length.
- Carlisle Papers - These highlight the very best of student papers from the Army War College.
- Letort Papers - Essays, retrospectives, or speeches of interest to the defense academic community.

- Colloquium Reports - For larger conferences SSI may produce a report on the proceedings.

- Colloquium Briefs - These two-to-four page briefs are produced after the colloquia with which we have co-sponsored or helped fund.

At the request of the Army leadership, SSI sometimes provides shorter analytical reports on pressing strategic issues. The distribution of these is usually limited.

Additionally, every year SSI compiles a Key Strategic Issues List (KSIL) based on input from the U.S. Army War College faculty, the Army Staff, the Joint Staff, the unified and specified commands, and other Army organizations. This is designed to guide the research of SSI, the U.S. Army War College, and other Army-related strategic analysts.

SSI analysts publish widely outside of the Institute's own products. They have written books for Cambridge University Press, Princeton University Press, University Press of Kansas, Duke University Press, Praeger, Frank Cass, Rowman, and Littlefield and Brassey's. They have contributed chapters to many other books including publications from the Brookings Institution, Jane's Defence Group, and the Center for Strategic and International Studies. SSI analysts have written articles for *Foreign Affairs, International Security, Survival, Washington Quarterly, Orbis, The National Interest, Current History, Political Science Quarterly, Joint Force Quarterly, Parameters, The Journal of Politics, Security Studies, Journal of Strategic Studies, Jane's Intelligence Review, Occasional Papers* of the Woodrow Wilson Center, *Contemporary Security Policy, Defense Analysis, Military Operations Research, Strategic Review, Military Review, National Security Studies Quarterly, Journal of Military History, War in History, War & Society, The Historian, Infantry Magazine, The World and I, Aerospace Historian, Central Asian Security, Asian Survey, SAIS Review, China Quarterly, Comparative Politics, Journal of Political and Military Sociology, Small Wars and Insurgencies, Georgetown Journal of International Affairs, Special Warfare, Comparative Strategy, Korean Journal of Defense Analysis, Journal of East Asian Studies, World Affairs, Problems of Post-Communism, Conflict, Diplomatic History, Airpower Journal, Low*

Intensity Conflict and Law Enforcement, Politique Étranger, Allgemeine Schweizerische Militärzeitschrift, and *African Security Review.*

SSI also co-sponsors academic conferences to examine issues of importance to the Army, collaborating with some of the most prestigious universities in the country. Recent partners included Georgetown, Princeton, Harvard, MIT, Columbia, University of Chicago, University of Miami, Stanford, Georgia Tech, Johns Hopkins, and the Bush School of Government and Public Service at Texas A&M University.

Named in honor of the 34th President of the United States, the **Dwight D. Eisenhower National Security Series** seeks to explore new ways to employ more effectively our Nation's capabilities to meet the range of security challenges we face in the 21st century.

The Series was established in 2002 by the Chief of Staff of the United States Army to address the critical security issues of our time. It is a full year of programs and activities that engage and involve all facets of the national security community. News media, corporate and economic policy representatives, academia and think tanks, all departments of the U.S. government, nongovernmental and international organizations, the diplomatic community, members of Congress and their staffs, foreign officials, and specialists are all invited and have the opportunity to contribute. Indeed, to ensure diversity of opinion and balanced inquiry, the Army partners with co-sponsors from each of these sectors in the conceptualization, planning, and execution of each Eisenhower Series event. This approach is a more effective means of exploring the complex security issues of the 21st century.

The Series culminates annually with the Dwight D. Eisenhower National Security Conference in Washington, DC. At the conference, a distinguished array of national security decisionmakers will assemble for 2 days to make presentations, participate in panel discussions, and field questions in a setting which promotes extensive discourse focused on a single unifying theme. The 2006 theme is "National Security for a New Era—The Evolution of Cooperation, Competition, and Conflict."